COMPLAINT

BIG IDEAS

General editor: Lisa Appignanesi

As the twenty-first century moves through its tumultuous first decade, we need to think about our world afresh. It's time to revisit not only politics, but our passions and preoccupations, and our ways of seeing the world. The Big Ideas series challenges people who think about these subjects to think in public, where soundbites and polemics too often provide sound and fury but little light. These books stir debate and will continue to be important reading for years to come.

Other titles in the series include:

COMPLAINT

FROM MINOR MOANS TO PRINCIPLED PROTESTS

Julian Baggini

PROFILE BOOKS

First published in Great Britain in 2008 by
PROFILE BOOKS LTD
3A Exmouth House
Pine Street
London EC1R 0JH
www.profilebooks.com

1 3 5 7 9 10 8 6 4 2

Typeset in Minion by MacGuru Ltd
info@macguru.org.uk
Printed and bound in Italy by Legoprint

The moral right of the author has been asserted.

A CIP catalogue record for this book is available from the
British Library.

ISBN 978 1 84668 057 1

CONTENTS

So I have not said to my people: 'Get rid of your discontent.'
Rather, I have tried to say that this normal and healthy
discontent can be channeled into the creative outlet of
nonviolent direct action.

Martin Luther King, letter from Birmingham Jail, 16 April 1963

www.thecomplaintbook.com

INTRODUCTION

Think of the word 'complaint' and you're likely to conjure images of moaning, whining rants about mainly trivial matters: the trains don't run on time, people are so rude these days, there's nowhere to park, there's nothing on the television. Complaining has become a pastime of the resigned and the nostalgic. It has even become something of a leisure activity. In the UK the best-selling book one recent Christmas was the self-explanatory *Is It Just Me or Is Everything Shit?*, while the year before the runaway hit was *Eats, Shoots & Leaves*, a protracted complaint against the decline of proper grammar. The TV series *Grumpy Old Men*, which comprised people complaining to camera, was such a success it spawned the sequels *Grumpy Old Women* and *Grumpy Old Holidays*, as well as spin-off books and even a touring stage show. Even indie rock bands have discovered that being world-weary is cooler than getting angry, with Blur releasing an album called *Modern Life Is Rubbish* and The Kaiser Chiefs scoring a hit with their song 'Everything Is Average Nowadays'. Complaining has become synonymous with moaning.

It needn't be this way. At the root of every complaint is a sense that things are not as they ought to be. To complain is to speak out against this, and we can do so petulantly, aggressively, calmly, pointlessly or constructively. It does not even matter whether we are truly upset by what we perceive to be wrong. Many people are never happier than when they get the opportunity to complain, while others are deeply unhappy with how things are, but just accept it. Complaint occurs when we refuse to accept that things are wrong and try to do something about it, even if that something is no more than articulating the fault.

Although the precondition for complaint is a belief that things are not as they should be, the mere recognition and expression of this fact are not enough for a fully formed complaint to be born. For example, a stoic may believe that it is important to accept the imperfection of the world, and so to recognise that things are not as they ought to be would, for her, be not to complain but simply to describe. Likewise, a committed pessimist may also like frequently to comment on what's wrong with everything, but again this is not really complaint because it lacks a *non-acceptance* of what is wrong.

There is an additional final component of complaint which is hard to pin down. Complaint is doubly transitive: you don't just complain *about* something, you complain *to* someone or something. However, as a criterion for identifying genuine complaints, this is hard to apply, because often what we direct our complaints to is entirely abstract: God, the fates, fortune or just the universe. Such generalised directedness can be hard to identify, but I think we can tell, in our own cases at least, the difference between merely thinking that something is wrong and hurling our rage about it into the empty air, as though someone should be listening and taking note.

Complaint can therefore be defined as *a directed expression of a refusal or inability to accept that things are not as they ought to be*. The definition is a little loose and almost certainly has exceptions, but, unlike many philosophers, I'm happy with that. Language is more flexible than logic, and if you want to describe the world as it is, rather than remake it in a form fit for logicians, you have to be prepared to live with a certain amount of ambiguity. It also seems to me that complaint is a particularly indeterminate concept. Consider, for instance, the familiar scenario when someone appears to be having a moan, and they are told to stop complaining. 'I'm not complaining,' comes the reply, 'I'm just *saying*.' Often the person really is complaining and doesn't want to admit it, but the very concept of complaint opens up the wiggle-room for plausible denial. This is, I think, because the features of directedness and non-acceptance which are central to complaint admit of many degrees. It can therefore be hard to know how much our expressions that things are not right contain either or both.

Even if you prefer a slightly different definition, it should be plain that what we complain about can be trivial or profoundly important. All major social advances have started with a complaint. Emmeline Pankhurst and the suffragettes, Martin Luther King and the civil rights campaign, Nelson Mandela and the anti-apartheid movement: the changes they brought about all began with a complaint that the status quo was wrong and needed to be changed.

The act of complaining is hence not what is fundamental to complaint: it is a symptom, not the disease itself. Just as the severity of a medical complaint should be measured not by how loudly it draws attention to itself but by the extent to which the body really is damaged, so we should not mistake the loudness of a complaint for its seriousness.

Complaint has a noble history. It has driven human society forward and led to the abolition of systemic injustice. That it is now primarily associated with inconsequential moans and frivolous litigation is a travesty. This is the main complaint of this book. For instance, the grievance culture that infects America and Britain is just the latest and most striking example of how complaint can go wrong, and I will be examining it in some detail in the final chapter.

I want to reclaim complaint for the forces of progress and wrestle it from the hands of the lawyers who see it as simply a means to personal gain, and from those of the doom-mongers and naysayers who believe that nothing can be done except whinge. To do this I need to look at what we complain about, why we complain, what our complaints say about us, and whether we should complain more, less or just differently.

Although my claim is that complaint is at the heart of many genuinely important things, I do not wish to neglect the more mundane moans of everyday life. It is a long-standing belief of mine that the profound and the trivial live side by side, that human beings are not separated into their nobler and baser parts but are a thorough mixture of the two. In the details of everyday life we often see the fractal patterns that mirror the larger, most important contours of our nature. So later in the book I will be turning to some observations about quotidian complaints, with some help from a specially devised survey, the results of which make some intriguing suggestions about how our complaints reflect who we are. I would not go so far as to say that complaint provides the key with which we can unlock the hidden secrets of human existence, but it is certainly a lens worth looking through, one which puts into sharp focus aspects of life which usually appear to the mind's eye as a vague blur.

What I will not be discussing is what might be called insincere complaint. Research psychologists and sociologists have generally neglected complaint, but the few who have examined it have identified many types of complaining behaviour which are not really about things being wrong at all. For example, we may complain about the price of opera tickets to signal that we're rich and cultured, or we may join in a collective complaint to identify ourselves with a group.[1] One particularly vivid example of insincere complaint was the newspaper columnist who complained that morning sex with her new four-times-a-night boyfriend made her driving worse. Poor woman. No comprehensive account could ignore such instrumental uses of complaint, but for my purposes I want to focus on cases where the sense of things not being right and our expression of dissatisfaction with that are essentially sincere.

What I'm offering is a kind of meta-complaint: that people tend to complain about the wrong things for the wrong reasons and that, as a result, complaining has been debased. But in so doing, I hope to demonstrate that complaint can be constructive. Indeed, our ability to complain is part and parcel of what makes us human.

1

THE NOBLE HISTORY OF COMPLAINT

Divine complaint

What was the first complaint in human history? For those who believe Genesis is a historical record there is a factual answer to this question. For those who believe it is merely a myth, that answer is still of interest because it reveals something about how we have understood complaint in the development of humankind.

When God created the world, he saw that it was good. Everything was as it should have been, and there was hence nothing to complain about. Adam and Eve, in their original state, were incapable of complaint for they did not know the difference between good and evil, right and wrong, and without any sense of this, how could one even conceive of the idea that things are not as they ought to be? There is no awareness of 'should' in a prelapsarian state, only of 'is'.

The serpent was the first character in the story to suggest that all was not well in Eden, but even he did not complain. He merely gave Eve an alternative story to the one God offered. 'Ye shall not surely die: for God doth know that in the day ye eat thereof, then your eyes shall be opened, and ye shall be as gods, knowing good and evil.'

What was Eve to do? She did not know the difference between good and evil, so by definition she could not have known that she ought not to do what the serpent suggested. To have known eating the fruit was wrong she would have to have known what she could have known only after having eaten it.

And so, naïve and innocent, she naturally helped herself, as the serpent suggested, and then gave Adam a bite.

Immediately the possibility of complaint arose, since for the first time the couple were able to see that things were not as they should have been: they were naked. But still they did not complain, they 'sewed fig leaves together, and made themselves aprons'. Quite wisely, they knew that there is no point in complaining if a simple action can solve a problem.

The first complaint came not from Adam, Eve or the Devil, but from God himself. 'Who told thee that thou wast naked? Hast thou eaten of the tree, whereof I commanded thee that thou shouldest not eat?' God got mad, and then he got even. He gave women pain in childbirth and a duty of obedience to their husbands, and he expelled both of them from Eden, to a life of toil. Why? Because 'man is become as one of us, to know good and evil.' Humanity's crime was to become too much like God. It was bad enough that we knew the difference between good and evil; God could not risk that we would gain immortality too. Hence, 'lest he put forth his hand, and take also of the tree of life, and eat, and live for ever', God banished us.

Far be it for me to argue with the divine creator, but there do seem to be serious issues surrounding the justice of all this. Leaving these to one side, the myth describes something very important about the role of complaint in human life. Complaining is both supremely divine and human. God complains first, yet it is only after we become fallen beings, and hence human beings in the full sense, that we can do the same.

This is the paradox of the fall. It is often related as a tale of paradise lost, as though we would all be much better-off if it had never happened. Yet it is obvious that Adam and Eve before the fall were more like overgrown children than true, reflective adults. We say that ignorance is bliss, but without the capacity to understand right and wrong we would be less than fully human. The fall is not what ruined us; it is what made us.

God didn't like us eating from Eden's tree because it made us better, more like him, and so he had to resort to throwing his superior power about to keep us in our place. Knowing the difference between right and wrong enables us to complain when things are wrong. The Bible is full of stories that suggest God has never been very happy for us to use this ability. Theologically speaking, complaining is bad for us.

Despite being the most upright man alive, Job, for instance, has miseries piled upon him with the acquiescence of God, who wants to win a bet with the Devil. 'My soul is weary of my life', says Job, but 'I will leave my complaint upon myself; I will speak in the bitterness of my soul'. The lesson of Job's story is clear: no matter how miserable our lot is, we should never complain to our creator about it. 'Wilt thou also disannul my judgement? Wilt thou condemn me, that thou mayest be righteous? Hast thou an arm like God? Or canst thou thunder with a voice like him?'

Similarly, the Christian New Testament, although it commands us to be charitable, teaches us not to try to alter the basic injustices of life. We must render unto Caesar and accept the poor will be with us always. Christ didn't lead a terrestrial rebellion to overthrow the Romans, which is why, according to the legend, the people turned against him. 'My kingdom is not of this world', he testified at his trial. St Paul even encourages slaves to know their place and keep in it: 'Exhort servants to be obedient unto their own masters, and to please them well in all things; not answering again.'

The great success of Christianity was that it made not complaining seem so natural when, to an outside observer, a world in which millions of people live in misery should be up in arms at the deity who created them with so little apparent concern for their happiness. That is certainly how the author of western Europe's first overtly atheist document saw it. Jean Meslier (1664–1729) was a rural French priest who wrote a secret testament, published only after his death, in which he argued against the beliefs of the Church he purportedly served. What kept him from resigning was partly fear of being burned at the stake, but also a sense of service to his parishioners, whose welfare he tried to promote with incredible dedication.

In his play about Meslier, *The Last Priest*, David Walter Hall captured Meslier's realisation of how religion had managed to distort his parishioners' sense of justice:

> They don't complain, well they don't complain to me. I wonder what they pray about, whether they're all at home complaining, as they rightfully should be, as I would be. And why aren't they knocking on my door, with a disgruntled message to take to their creator?[2]

Another pioneering atheist thinker, Friedrich Nietzsche, argued that Christianity glorified moral resignation so much that its ethic deserved the name of 'slave morality'. The religion spoke to the poor, the weak and the dispossessed, and, instead of encouraging them to overcome these limitations, it taught that being at the bottom of the pile was virtuous. People should not complain about social injustice; they should take heart from the fact that they will inherit the earth and it will be the fat rich who struggle to squeeze through heaven's gates.

Of course, Christ's teaching had a strong social message, but it was based on voluntary aid, not resistance to oppressive power. He with two coats should give one to a person who has none, but we should certainly not seize the excess clothing of the over-attired in the name of redistribution of wealth.

Indeed, the Catholic Church in particular has a poor track record on resistance to despicable regimes, as long as it is allowed to continue to serve its higher authority. It supported fascism in Italy and Spain and signed a concordat with the Nazi government in Germany in 1933. In Rwanda, Catholics were implicated in assisting the Hutus in the genocide of the Tutsis, but far from condemning them, the Pope's only direct intervention was to appeal for a stay of execution for those found guilty of these horrendous crimes.[3] The ease with which the Church can accommodate itself to tyrannical regimes would seem puzzling in the light of its central moral message, but the mystery vanishes once you understand that it does not see its duty as being to challenge earthly rulers.

The negative proof of this thesis, at least as far as the Catholic Church is concerned, comes with the rise of liberation theology in Latin America, which saw Christ not only as a spiritual redeemer but as the liberator of the oppressed. For a short while, after the Second Vatican Council of 1962–65, the movement found favour with the Catholic hierarchy. But this was a bit of a blip, and John Paul II in particular turned against it, with Benedict XVI following in his footsteps. The message is clear: it is heresy to see the Christian faith as being more concerned with worldly change than spiritual transformation.

Fortunately, the reverence religious believers have for their sacred texts is honoured more in the breach than in the observance. Many devout people have worked selflessly for social change. Christians may revere the Bible, but those who truly live by it are atypical, and somewhat frightening. No matter what believers actually say and do, one central message of the Abrahamic faiths' holy books is all too clear, if you care to look: do not complain, but accept God's will.

Religion

Complaint is a secular, humanist act. It is resistance against the idea, promulgated by religion, that suffering is our divinely ordained lot and that we can do no more than put up with it piously. It is an insistence that justice must not wait for the next life but must be attained here. It is the result not just of seizing knowledge of the difference between good and evil, but of actually using that understanding to challenge what rulers and priestly castes have always told us is the natural order. Religion laments the fact that we ate Eden's apple and thus had our eyes opened to the grounds of complaint. Humanism celebrates it.

All the traditional teachings of the main religions conform to this pattern, even though their followers have on many occasions taken a stand against earthly injustice. Buddhism is perhaps most obviously antithetical to complaint. The Buddha teaches that nirvana lies in freeing ourselves from all striving and attachment to material conditions. In particular, Buddhism teaches that suffering is a part of life and that if you set out to avoid it within this mortal realm, you will inevitably fail. To end the cycle of suffering that is life and death, one starts by accepting its inevitability. Release is found not by changing the world but by changing yourself. Like the stoic philosophers, Buddhism teaches that you can't completely control what happens to you, but you can be the master of how you react to it. 'As a man who has no wound on his hand cannot be hurt by the poison he may carry in his hand, since poison hurts not where there is no wound, the man who has no evil cannot be hurt by evil', says the Buddha in the *Dhammapada*.[4]

For example, when the Buddha talks about abandoning sorrow, he talks about 'six causes', but none of them is an imperfection in the world that you should strive to change. Rather you should ignore them, avoid them, abandon or restrain the desires that lead to them, use things such as food and drink properly so that they don't cause any sorrow to arise, develop yourself so that you are above such suffering, or endure.[5] Strikingly absent is any talk of the cause as we would understand that term politically. Consider how this teaching would apply to someone suffering because of homophobia. The advice would be: avoid or ignore homophobes; abandon or restrain the desire which leads to the homophobia, which could be the sexual desire itself or the desire to have one's sexuality publicly accepted; use one's sexuality in such a way that it doesn't lead to a homophobic response, which sounds like staying in the closet; develop yourself so that you rise above the bigots; or put up with it. Complaining that homophobia is wrong and campaigning to end it just don't make the list.

The monks who led the protests against the Burmese junta in 2007 may seem to provide a clear counter-example, but in fact they are the exception that proves the rule, in the proper sense of the expression. The role of the monks was so noteworthy precisely because they had renounced the secular world, and so their involvement in politics was an exceptional occurrence. They were moved to act as they did because of the centrality of compassion in Buddhist ethics. The suffering of the Burmese people had become too great for them to remain silent. Extreme circumstances therefore required them to suspend their usual detachment from worldly affairs. Hence their remarkable protests actually highlighted the extent to which they usually do not complain strongly about terrestrial injustice.

The reasons for this are theologically coherent, even if they are philosophically suspect. Buddhism teaches that the self is an illusion, that you are merely the sum of all thoughts and experiences that the various parts of yourself have. 'There is no self residing in body and mind', taught the Buddha, 'but the co-operation of the conformations produces what people call a person.'[6] Nirvana requires that we give up all attachment to the self, because if we don't, we remain attached to a fiction. Such a dissolution of the self is the supreme expression of a belief system that believes it foolish to attach any real importance to matters of the world. 'You too shall pass away. Knowing this, how can you quarrel?'[7] To complain is thus to reveal that one has failed to realise that all things pass, and that one is mentally fighting illusions.

Islam too teaches us to accept our lot rather than fight against it. The word 'Islam' means submission, to God's will. I got a crash course in what this meant soon after the Asian tsunami, when I took part in a televised discussion about the 'problem of evil': how could a good God allow such pointless suffering? I was used to debating this issue with Christians, who resort to complicated 'theodicies' to resolve the problem. But the Muslim woman in our discussion said that in her religion, you are taught not even to ask why God would allow such a thing. If something happens, it is God's will, and that is all you need to know.

The Qu'ran certainly says that all that happens, good or bad, is God's will. All life's sufferings have a purpose: 'We shall test your steadfastness with fear and famine, with loss of life and property and crops. Give good news to those who endure with fortitude; who in adversity say: "We belong to Allah, and to him we shall return"' (2:155–6). An example of 'unjust and foolish thoughts about Allah' in the Qu'ran is: 'They complain: "Had we any say in the matter, we should not have been slain here."' What we are told we should say in return is: 'Had you stayed in your homes, those of you who were destined to be slain would have gone to their graves nevertheless; for it was Allah's will to test your faith and courage' (3:154–5). Believers can certainly petition God, but we should not fool ourselves that anyone other than God can remedy our complaints: 'If Allah afflicts you with evil, none can remove it but he' (6:17).[8] Once again, believing that things ought not to be as bad as they are is impious.

Such a belief may be comforting in times of disaster, but believers do not apply the principle uniformly. It is clearly not God's will that Palestinians should be denied a proper homeland by the Israelis, for example. The rule seems to be that things we don't like but cannot change are simply God's will; but for other things we don't like it is God's will that we change them.

The claim that religion is an enemy of complaint may seem to be instantly refuted by the numerous historical occasions when the devout have taken up the struggle against injustice. But how people have chosen to act says nothing about the logical implications of what they profess to believe. The fact that there are Christian socialists does not prove that Christ preached socialism. Christianity tells us to turn the other cheek, yet countless wars have been waged in Christ's name. Does this aggression in any way negate the truth that the gospels preach peace?

In the same way, the fact that many believers have campaigned for change is no refutation of the claim that their teachings at the very least tend away from complaint and towards compliance. That believers refuse to confine their ambitions to an afterlife merely confirms that human beings find renunciation of their evident mortality harder than suits the priests. Logically, the rewards of eternity should make the sufferings of this all too brief life seem as trivial as a small itch.

That they do not suggests that belief in the divine runs shallower than we might think.

There is an old saying that there are no atheists in foxholes, meaning that, when their backs are against the wall, everyone will pray to some higher power. This is demonstrably false. In *Touching the Void* the atheist climber Joe Simpson tells the incredible story of how he managed to drag his injured body off a mountain and survive against the odds. Brought up a devout Catholic, Simpson says, in the film adaptation, 'I always wondered, if things really hit the fan, whether I would, under pressure, turn around and say a few Hail Marys, and say "get me out of here". It never once occurred to me.'

A more persuasive saying might be that there are no theists at funerals. The grief we involuntarily feel when we say goodbye to loved ones only makes sense if on some level we truly think we have lost them for ever.

All religions and belief systems can be understood as reactions to the imperfection of human life. You can accept it and thus renounce life, as the Buddhists and stoics do. You can believe that the imperfection is to be suffered, for perfection is to come later, as most theists do. Alternatively, you can fight it.

This spirit is captured in Dylan Thomas's poem 'Do Not Go Gentle Into That Good Night', in which the poet beseeches his dying father to 'rage, rage against the dying of the light'. It is in many ways a futile plea. All sensible atheists accept that death is inevitable and we have to come to terms with it in some way. Passive submission, however, is not the only way to accept the limits of human power. What Thomas's poem reflects is not the impossible desire to keep breathing for ever, but the fight to make every heartbeat felt. If you truly value human life, you cannot resign yourself to accepting all its imperfections without any struggle. When things are not as they should, or could, be, that struggle starts with a complaint.

The great complainers

Social progress has been achieved in human history because people have complained about contemporary injustice and then, crucially, been willing to do something about it. The link between complaint and action is critical, because today we tend to see complaining as a self-contained, purely symbolic act. People spend whole nights in pubs complaining about the treachery of politicians, for example, but if you ask them why they don't stand for election themselves, the answer is almost invariably, 'What's the point?' But you could ask the same of any complaint without subsequent action. Complaining is only useless if done by itself. At its best, it provides the impetus to do something significant.

Most of the key moments in the development of modern societies began with legitimate complaints. Magna Carta has a mythical status in the history of England, despite the fact that few actually know what it was and what it said, an ignorance immortalised in Tony Hancock's line 'Does Magna Carta mean nothing to you? Did she die in vain?'

Magna Carta was not a single document, and its actual effect on the power of the king was limited. However, it is remembered as a symbol for how a widespread complaint was finally resolved. The monarch had too much power, including the authority to imprison anyone he wished. Magna Carta represents the citizens' success in limiting their ruler's power by law. That it mainly helped barons rather than the wider populace is forgotten.

The belief that the people have a right to complain and should not suffer injustice in silence is implicit in all movements for social change. In the mid-nineteenth century the Chartists, for instance, complained that the country was being governed in a fundamentally undemocratic way. Only a small minority could vote, and the rules for eligibility varied from town to town. This meant that there were many 'rotten boroughs', where fewer than 100 people would be able to choose who to send to parliament, while over half a million citizens in Manchester, Leeds, Birmingham and Sheffield had not a single MP between them. You could become a member of parliament only if you owned property, and because parliamentarians were not paid, only people with private incomes could realistically take on the task. Voting was not even conducted under a secret ballot. The Chartists did not succeed immediately, but they were pivotal in raising the importance of electoral reform, and in time their key aims were achieved.

The USA can trace the story of its independence to the first complaint of 'no taxation without representation'. Slavery would never have been abolished, had no one seen fit to complain about its injustice. The Quakers were at the forefront of campaigns for abolition, as they have been in many social justice issues. It is no surprise that a dissenting religion with a lax stance on the authority of the Bible was ahead of more orthodox denominations which took longer to see the injustice of bondage.

The list goes on. When the suffragette movement started there was no shortage of people who insisted that voteless women had nothing to complain about. Feminists who dared to question endemic patriarchy were similarly mocked and told their complaints were groundless. All emancipatory movements begin with complaints that are dismissed. Getting people to accept them as legitimate is key to their achieving success.

Complaint is therefore not a trivial matter of petty moans. To complain is not only to be fully human: it is to defy the divine. It is what spurs us to squeeze the most out of our short, mortal lives, rather than resign ourselves to our lot. Without it no progressive social change would ever come about.

At least, that is complaint at its best. At its worst it is a useless waste of energy, a futile cry against the inevitable, a refusal to accept reality for what it is. How is it that something so important can in another guise be so pointless? To answer that question we need to understand the myriad ways in which complaining can be abused and misused.

2

IMPOSSIBLE COMPLAINT

Right complaint requires considering the possibility of change. Reinhold Niebuhr's serenity prayer captures the heart of it:

> God grant me the serenity
> To accept the things I cannot change;
> Courage to change the things I can;
> And wisdom to know the difference.

The wisdom required, however, is the knowledge not just of the difference between what can and can't be changed, but of what *ought* to be changed. Mention of God aside, agreeing with the serenity prayer is easy, since in abstract terms it's platitudinous. It's how you put the flesh on its bones which counts. My contention is that religion has tended to overestimate the extent to which things cannot or should not be changed. But to underestimate it would be just as much of an error.

Wrong complaints can take one of three forms: they can be about things that can't be changed, about those that shouldn't, or about those which neither can nor should be changed. Right complaints are simply those about things which can and should be changed.

However, there are always many more ways of being wrong than there are of being right. So it is with complaint. Hence to understand right complaint it serves us well to contrast it with numerous wrong complaints. If we want to reclaim complaint as a progressive, positive force, it is necessary to identify why it is that complaint so often fails to meet up to this high expectation. To do this, we need a taxonomy of wrong complaint.

In this chapter I'm going to look at complaints which are wrong because they concern things that cannot be changed, while in the next I'll turn to things we should not try to change.

What we can't change

On inspirational posters, tea towels and web sites we are assured that the only thing that stands between us and our goals is negative thinking. 'With love and patience, nothing is impossible', said the Japanese Buddhist Daisaku Ikeda. 'It is often merely for an excuse that we say things are impossible', agreed the seventeenth-century French writer François de la Rochefoucauld. 'The only way to discover the limits of the possible is to go beyond them into the impossible', inspired Arthur C. Clarke. 'To the timid and hesitating everything is impossible because it seems so', chided Sir Walter Scott. 'The Difficult is that which can be done immediately; the Impossible that which takes a little longer', said George Santayana. You get the picture.

To respond to this barrage of positive thinking and unlimited aspiration with the suggestion that some things just can't be done sounds heretically negative. Who could be so cold and pessimistic as to suggest that, actually, sometimes you have to put up with imperfection and get on with it? Well, me. And William Faulkner, who wrote, 'All of us failed to match our dreams of perfection. So I rate us on the basis of our splendid failure to do the impossible.'

Unless the authors of the inspirational quotes I cited were actually just stupid, Faulkner's comparative cynicism must be very close in essence to what they really meant. No one literally believes that nothing is impossible. If Daisaku Ikeda believes that it is only because of a lack of love and patience that I can't kick a football like David Beckham, then he's not wise but delusional. Although Scott believed the timid and hesitating found everything impossible, he'd surely agree that only the arrogant and foolish believe nothing is.

Fighting against the impossible makes sense in two ways. First, in order to know the difference between what is impossible and what merely seems so, you have to try to do things which apparently can't be done. Sometimes the attempt will confirm the real impossibility of the ambition, as was the case with alchemists who tried to turn base metals into gold. On other occasions we will be pleasantly surprised.

Second, the impossible can sometimes be used as a target to aim at, even though we should not kid ourselves that we will ever reach it. This is most evidently useful when the impossibility in question is perfection. Artists, artisans, cooks and sportspeople all aim for perfection, even though they know that at best it can be achieved only in part or fleetingly.

It is often said that it is better to aim for perfection and miss than it is to aim for something less, because it is better to fall short of a higher standard than a lower one. I'm not so sure. The rule seems to hold fine when the outcome is merely the difference between doing well and doing better. But when the stakes are winning or losing, or life and death, it seems to me that pragmatism – that most loathed but necessary of concepts – has to come into it. In sport, for instance, you can find plenty of examples of teams or individuals who tried to play the perfect game and were undone by opponents who took a more practical approach. The victorious Greek European Championship football team of 2004, which beat Portugal to lift the trophy, is one of the most striking examples of how a well-drilled team of generally mediocre talents can overcome more gifted opposition. I am also somewhat concerned by the psychological weakness that the lust for perfection entails. There is no logical reason why we must temporarily convince ourselves we can do the impossible in order to do our best, but psychologically, this seems to be an almost universal truth. My own personal motto is 'less than perfect, more than good enough'. I accept from the start that I'm not going to be perfect, but I push myself by trying not to settle for the merely adequate. I find this more motivating than trying to convince myself I can be the greatest, because I don't think I could hold on to that illusion for too long. If I make it my goal, therefore, I'm going to be frequently downhearted, dejected and discouraged. As it is, when I see faults in myself, or others point them out, I can accept them and try to learn from them more easily than if awareness of these failings had shattered an over-inflated self-image.

The idea that we should not accept anything as impossible is therefore true only insofar as it does not mean what it literally says. Realism does have to enter the picture at some stage, and realism involves accepting that there are limits on what we can do, as individuals and as a species. Right complaint needs to take this on board too: there is no point in protesting that things are not as they ought to be if they can't be any different.

That is why complaining about the inevitable or unchangeable is a species of wrong complaint. Perhaps the most common form of this is complaint directed against the fallibility and unpredictability of human nature. This has a significant political import. Historically, many on the left have complained about greed, corruption and inequality in society, and justifiably so. However, you have to be very careful how precisely you direct that complaint. If you think that things could be organised better so as to reduce inequality and to provide checks and balances against the darker side of human nature, then it seems to me that nothing you are protesting about is impossible to change. But if you blame the system as the root cause of all base motives among people, then your complaint is misguided, for what you are saying needs to change is not just the system but human nature itself. Get the politics right, the theory goes, and you just won't see people behaving badly. As people optimistically believed in the throes of almost every socialist revolution, individuals will gladly work for the common good with no thought for self-interest because they will realise that the common good is their good too. In such a society cheating and greed would be pointless.

This prediction has been shown to be hopelessly wrong. Collectivisation in the Soviet Union, for example, led to economic stagnation, not stimulation, while one's standing within the Communist Party provided plenty of opportunity for old-fashioned greed, competition and self-interest to persist. However, a remarkable number of people still believe it is true and will argue that the failures of the various socialist revolutions to date show only that no one has yet created a pure enough Utopia for such a selfless society to take root. The complaint is that no state has been socialist enough, but this is wrong complaint, because no state could ever be pure enough to transform human nature as much as the theory requires.

People object to this diagnosis on the basis that it is pessimistic and that it rests on an untenable view about the rigidity of human nature. The pessimism charge is neither here nor there. Any view can be described as pessimistic if compared with another which makes undeliverable promises. Furthermore I don't think it is pessimistic, because it still allows for many other options to make a better world.

Nor do you need to be committed to a view of human nature in which everything is biologically hard-wired. Indeed, to believe that nothing in human nature is alterable is as blinkered as believing that everything is. Any credible view of the pliability of human nature has to accept that change is possible only within certain limits. Those constraints do not merely check our pretensions to angelhood: they also save us from all ending up as devils. Empathy, for example, is sufficiently finite in humans for us to predict with some certainty that on average people will care more about themselves and people close to them than about strangers. But the existence of that empathy also means that eradicating all feeling for strangers, although achievable in the short run, will never be universal or permanent. Believe in the infinite malleability of human nature and it is true you can imagine a communal Utopia to come, but you also leave open the possibility of forging a racist and fascist future.

An alternative way of saving the Utopian dream is to claim that human nature is not infinitely malleable but fundamentally good, and that only the corrupting effects of society conceal this fact. If you like to believe things without any shred of evidence, you can maintain this. But anthropologists have found that the natural state of human beings is not to be wild, free and pacific. For a start, every human society is just that – a *society* of some sort – and so even talking about humans uncorrupted by society is confused. If you mean uncorrupted by modern, capitalist society, then the argument is just as weak, because pre-industrial societies are still generally hierarchical, misogynistic and not immune to violent conflict, internally or with external enemies. Studies of contemporary hunter–gatherer societies suggest that 90 per cent of them go to war every year, and that over a quarter of adult males meet violent ends.[9]

The truth about human nature is neither base nor ignoble. The primatologist Frans de Waal makes this case eloquently by comparing us to our nearest relatives, chimpanzees and bonobos.[10] Of course, you cannot deduce anything about human nature simply by observing apes, but De Waal convincingly argues that we can conclude that these animals reflect aspects of human nature because when we observe them we experience recognition. We don't assume or deduce that these apes are like us in many ways: we *see* it. And what we see is neither all good nor all bad. We are co-operative in some ways, competitive in others. Pecking orders emerge in all groups, though some are more hierarchical than others. Males and females have different priorities, though that does not mean that overall one has more power than the other. You don't need to study apes to see that this is also true of human beings; you just need to look at human societies without prejudice.

Wrong complaint against the corrupting power of society, based on a naïve view of human goodness, has had disastrous consequences. Reforms based on right complaint – against the disenfranchisement of women, working people and ethnic minorities – have led to good outcomes, because the problems were correctly diagnosed. Reforms based on wrong complaint, based on a faulty diagnosis, have led to bad outcomes, because the premises for the changes were unsustainable falsehoods. Power was handed over to representatives of the proletariat on the assumption that they would not be as self-serving as the bourgeoisie they overthrew. Factories and farms were collectivised in the belief that people would be more productive than they were when they were mere employees, alienated from their labour. It was thought that status would cease to be important, even though no movement in human history has ever granted more status to the likes of Lenin, Mao, Che and Fidel than the revolutionary left.

I don't want to suggest that the socialist revolutions were complete mistakes. Often, if not usually, they did lead to societies in which life for the poor was better, and improving the lot of the worst-off in society should be a prime objective of political reform. The mistake is rather that of missed opportunity. That things are better than they were is not a good defence if things could easily have been better still. That these opportunities were missed is, I believe, largely due to the fact that legitimate complaint against present injustice was infected by misguided complaints about the source of human imperfection. Had those revolutionaries accepted that it is futile to complain about the mix of selfishness and altruism in human nature, they could have made reforms that would have taken better root in the people they claimed to be representing.

To complain that things ought to be different when they can never realistically be so is a waste of emotional energy, an infantile unwillingness to deal with the imperfection of the world. Such acceptance need not be passive. For example, the course of love rarely runs smooth. Does that mean we should not bother with love at all, or that when things go wrong we should just walk away, and shrug, 'I knew it!'? Of course not. The mature thing is to work with the imperfection. The same is true of political reform. We don't give up on it, nor do we accept the inevitability that it will all end in tears. Rather, we work in full knowledge of the limits of politics, knowing that good governance will never be perfect governance, and nor will it cure all the ills of the world. This can be hard to do, because many drawn to politics are by instinct idealists, who fear that to be anything else will be to give up and sell out.

This is a fear based on a simplistic black-and-white view of the world, which is itself a source of the kind of moral distortion which leads to wrong complaint.

Where the world is imperfect, the message is not 'stop complaining' but 'complain about what really can be changed'.

Moving on

The greatest impossibility of all is to change the past. Whatever we feel about what has happened, what is done is done, and nothing can undo it. Yet here we have another example of how complaint can be futile and how right complaint isn't so much about stopping our whinging as about directing our complaints into productive channels.

In the contemporary West we have become very bad at dealing with the past. On the one hand, it becomes a focus for nostalgia, which is enjoyable for its own sake but which rarely takes us forward. But as well as having a tendency to idealise the good times, we now seem in indecent haste to forget the bad ones. Sympathy for bad experiences doesn't last very long before we are told in exasperated tones that we must 'move on' or 'get over it'.

This is true of both the political and the personal. When in 1998 judge Baltasar Garzón of Spain issued an arrest warrant for General Augusto Pinochet of Chile for systematic torture, murder and illegal detention during his rule between 1973 and 1990, many said he should not be raking over old ground. Chile needed to move on, forget about it. The same argument has been used in post-Mussolini Italy, post-Franco Spain, post-Hitler Germany and virtually every other country where dictatorships have fallen. To complain that perpetrators of atrocities have gone unpunished is seen as vindictive and a waste of emotional energy.

In private life the imperative not to look back is taken even further. I was once told a story about someone's brother, who had been feeling down since splitting up with his long-term, live-in girlfriend. To cheer him up the brother and friend arranged for an obliging woman to arrive at his house in a long coat, only to reveal that underneath she was wearing nothing but lingerie. The idea was that they would then do what comes naturally. The morose man, however, far from being aroused, became even more upset. His brother couldn't understand this. 'Come on!' he said. 'It's been *three weeks!*'

This may be an extreme example, but being 'over it already' is taken as the hallmark of a strong, emotionally mature person. And it's easy to see why this view should prevail. There is indeed no point crying over spilt milk, and what's done truly is done. But those who complain wisely about the past are not suggesting otherwise. Rather, what they insist on is our coming to terms with what has happened and dealing with its aftermath.

Consider complaints about the legacy of slavery, for example. In 2007, on the anniversary of the passing of an act of parliament to abolish the slave trade in the United Kingdom, there were many debates about whether we should apologise for the past. Most thought we should not, for the same reasons that they thought we shouldn't complain about it either: it all happened a long time ago, and we cannot change it, nor should we feel responsible for it.

I think the focus on apology was misguided. Those who use the slave trade as a focus for contemporary complaint are often as uninterested in receiving a meaningless apology as anyone else. Rather, they believe that in at least two respects we have not dealt properly with the injustices of slavery. First, the racism and exploitation that enabled slavery to exist for so long are, it is claimed, still prevalent in contemporary society. As evidence, you can point to Western exploitation of developing world producers and the disproportionate failure of some ethnic minorities to rise to the top in various fields. Second, there is a legacy of slavery which has not been resolved, in that a lot of the wealth remains in the hands of ancestors of exploiters, while descendants of slaves are disproportionately poor.

Whether this case holds or not, it is a clear example of how legitimate complaints which can be resolved today can arise out of a consideration of past events which cannot be altered. That's why the idea that 'the past is past' and should just be forgotten is often too hasty. There is a difference between accepting the unalterable past and questioning the alterable present and future, which are only as they are because of the past.

In personal matters it is also not at all obvious that the past is always best forgotten. If someone has a deep love for another person, for example, and they then lose them or are betrayed, it is an entirely appropriate response to feel terrible for a long time. You may never again be as happy as you once were. We would suspect that the person who got up the day after such a trauma and announced that past is past and they're not at all miserable about it didn't actually have very deep feelings in the first place.

When a relationship ends, it can shatter your assumptions about who you are, your values and what can be expected of other people. If you don't then take the time to re-evaluate all these and simply try to soldier on, you risk learning nothing from your troubles and repeating the same mistakes. This process has a particular kind of complaint at its heart, one which comes close to the medical sense of the word. There is an acute sense that things should not have come to this, that there is something wrong with the world. And indeed there almost certainly is, but what is wrong is usually not that the break has happened but that the way things had been before was unsustainable. The purpose of focusing on the complaint is to understand why this was so. This is what enables you truly to 'move on', not denying that the past has any relevance for now.

We are temporal beings with pasts, presents and futures. In one sense we are firmly rooted to the now, but it is part of the complexity of human life that in another sense we need to live in all three tenses. Right complaint is part of what enables us to make the future better, for ourselves and for others, and although the past can never be changed, some such right complaints can be made only in reference to it.

Cathartic complaint

To see complaint as useless if it cannot alter the world would be to miss the point that the act of complaining can at least change the complainer. Most obviously, having a good moan can be extremely cathartic.

Consider, for example, the mistreated woman who gets together with her female friends to talk about what a bastard her former lover really is. Will this change him? Will it facilitate a reconciliation? Of course not. But will it make the woman feel better? Almost certainly.

As I have said, complaint springs from a sense that things are not as they should be, and although we cannot always remedy the flaws in reality, we can reassure ourselves that we are right to believe it is the world which is wrong. A cheated lover, for example, will often, quite irrationally, feel that she is to blame for her partner's bad behaviour, and that if somehow she had been different, tried harder or had bigger breasts, then she would have deserved and got better treatment. Getting together with a good friend and complaining about her now ex-boyfriend is a way of reconstructing her understanding of the world which enables her to see that fault lies outside herself. It is good for her to complain that things are not as they should be, even though she can't change them, because knowing why they are not right enables her to expunge her feelings of inadequacy and regain self-respect. This catharsis may need to be repeated several times until the poison of self-loathing is expelled, but as long as the focus is not on wanting things which cannot be changed to be different, that's fine.

On a day-to-day level most complaints serve no higher goal than that of reaffirming our sense of how things should really be. 'Isn't the weather awful?' we ask, knowing that agreement confirms that we are not mistaken to find it somewhat disheartening. 'Politicians are all a bunch of lying bastards!' we say, which, while not entirely true, affirms the perfectly laudable belief that honesty in politics should be our goal. 'There's nothing on the television', and so we are right to be bored by it. These are hardly the noblest forms of complaint, but in moderation they are at least reasonable.

The danger lies in using complaint for this purpose so frequently that it becomes a substitute for actually doing something. All specific complaints then lead to the point of resignation: 'What's the point?' Complaint ceases to be constructively cathartic and simply becomes an excuse to do nothing. 'Isn't the weather awful?' we ask, justifying a wasted afternoon sitting idly inside. 'Politicians are all a bunch of lying bastards!' we say, vindicating our own apathy. 'There's nothing on the television', but we don't turn it off. Complaint is genuinely cathartic only in those situations where change is not a possibility or a priority. Otherwise it can become part of the problem, not a helpful way to soothe it.

Recognising that there is a large class of cathartic complaints is a reminder that much of what we say is not about communicating information or making truth claims, which is what linguists and philosophers of language tend to focus on. Words are our most important social lubricants, and it is often more revealing to ask what someone is doing with their words than it is to ask what they mean by them. For instance, 'Nice day' is primarily a means of breaking the ice, not an attempt to sum up the prevailing meteorological conditions. People ask after your relatives not because they really want to know but because they want to increase intimacy. In the same way it would be a mistake to see many, if not most, complaints as being primarily about the contents of the sentences which form them. As I said in the introduction, my focus is on what I called sincere complaints, but in this sense of the word insincere ones are not necessarily useless or misguided.

~

Right complaint helps us to change something, which is why wrong complaint can arise when we fail to see that what we find hard to accept cannot be changed. Such wrong complaint either treats the impossible as possible or makes the possible seem impossible. In that sense wrong complaint is unrealistic and untruthful.

However, I have argued that it would be too simplistic to say that it is never right to complain about things we cannot change. First, we can at least change how we view the unchangeable. Second, as long as it is not used as a substitute for action we could take, complaint can at least be cathartic, reaffirming our sense that we are right to see that things are not ideal, even if we cannot do anything about them. But we do not achieve a genuine catharsis if our complaints actively promote inertia when what we really need to do is build momentum.

I do not draw these distinctions for their own sake, as a mere intellectual exercise. I believe that becoming aware of them may help us do some important psychological de-cluttering. Complaints easily fill our heads and use up emotional resources. Avoiding the wrong sort and focusing on the right kind is one way to stop our heads filling with distracting, unhelpful noise. The practice of right complaint and the avoidance of wrong complaint are thus parts, however small, of the practice of right living as a whole.

3

MISTAKEN COMPLAINT

I have argued that wrong complaint can be concerned with one or both of two groups of things: things that can't be changed and those that shouldn't. Although the category of things that *can't* be changed is not as straightforward as it sounds, it is at least less controversial than the category of things which *shouldn't* be changed. Not that the division between the two is neat: some of the forms of complaint I'll talk about in this chapter contain elements of the impossible as well as of the undesirable.

The debate over what should or should not be different is endless, because the number of things which could be different is endless. Rather than dip into this selectively, what I want to do is to identify the subcategories of wrong complaints into which misguided pleas for change can be slotted. Constructing a taxonomy of wrong complaint in this way is not only a more manageable task than identifying each member of the species; it also enables us to see patterns which a focus on particular exemplars alone would not. Like all new taxonomies, it will inevitably be incomplete, but it will at least provide a framework for others to amend and expand.

Contradictory complaints

A woman is eulogising her new lover. 'He's so laid back, it's amazing! He's just cool with how I am and tells me he doesn't want to change anything. What a relief after Ralf! And he's so reflective too. I love the way he really thinks about things when you talk to him, not like most guys, who just bore you with their opinions on anything. And he is so not vain.'

Several months later, the relationship is over. Why? 'He's so laid back he's virtually horizontal. I mean, you need some excitement in a relationship. He takes no interest in what I'm trying to achieve in my life or career: it's as though he wants to keep me preserved in aspic. And he's too damned quiet: I often can't get him to say clearly what he thinks. Sometimes I wonder if anything is going on his head at all. Plus, I wish he'd take a bit more care of his appearance and lose a few pounds.'

The sharpest blades are often on double-edged swords. To be charitable to the disappointed woman, it is reasonable enough that what suits someone at one time may not do so at another. I am not being inconsistent if I want quiet one day and noise the next. It is only if I complain about the noise and the quiet at the same time that my protests are contradictory.

However, although we are rarely so overtly confused that we literally demand incompatible things at the same time, in ways we do not notice we often do find ourselves doing just that. People's complaints about politics in advanced democracies often betray precisely this fault. On the one hand, you will hear people complain that politics is too tribal, and that the parties spend too much time fighting each other when they should be working together for the common good. Sometimes it seems that they disagree merely for the sake of it. Why shouldn't the opposition, for example, be willing to praise the government when it does something good? Likewise, why shouldn't the government simply adopt opposition policies, with thanks, when they have good ideas?

It all sounds very reasonable. But then the same people at another time will complain that the trouble with politics today is that there is no longer anything to choose between the parties. It's not just that they're all as bad as one another; it's that they also basically believe in capitalism, tempered by regulation, with taxation to fund essential social goods. They differ a little on the details, but there is no one arguing either for a much smaller government in a more libertarian state or for a truly ambitious socialist programme.

In other words, we complain both that the political parties differ unnecessarily and that they are not different enough. You can square the circle by arguing that the parties should be able both to offer radically different models for the running of society and to agree on many more specific policies than they do, but it is hard to believe that the sophisticated mental balancing act this entails is really what advocates of both complaints usually have in mind.

The contradiction arises from a failure to understand the pluralistic nature of social goods. There are many things that we value in private and public life. However, having more of one often requires that we have less of another. Rather than accept this as inevitable, we tend to believe it wrong whenever we have less of any given good that we could have more of.

In the politics example, the plural goods are those of co-operation and competition. Society does have something to gain from politicians working closely together, so that the best ideas can be shared and time isn't wasted on pointless disagreements. But it also has something to gain from diversity of opinion, since the more options available to the electorate and to governments, the more chance we have of finding the most effective ones.

The trouble is that more of one inevitably leads to less of the other. The necessity may not be logical, but it is certainly there in practice. A highly co-operative political culture, for example, will tend to foster greater conformity of opinion, for sociological and psychological reasons. It is well known that when people are exposed to a narrow range of similar views, 'group think' tends to lead them to accept more readily whatever the locally conventional wisdom happens to be. Conversely, a highly competitive political culture makes the free exchange of ideas between parties more difficult, because, again, the psychology and sociology of difference means that people become unwilling to acknowledge the virtues of their opponents.

In many ways modern representative democracy has been very successful in trying to balance these competing goods. Competition is fostered through elections, but co-operation is also required to pass legislation in parliament. The two factors are thus kept in a creative tension, without either being able to dominate the other.

Because both competition and co-operation are therefore compromised in some way, it is always possible to look at one in isolation and believe there is not enough of it. But this is the tragedy of a world in which goods are genuinely plural: we cannot have full measures of all of them. It is our failure to face up to this which leads us to make the contradictory complaint that there is both too much and too little difference between the parties.

There are numerous examples of how plural goods can give rise to contradictory complaints. Social mobility and increased opportunity are good things, but the better-educated tend to move around more, and so the result is a decline in the sense of community which comes from people living most of their lives in one place. But the same people complain about both lack of educational opportunity and the decline in traditional communities. Likewise, there are complaints about those left behind by increased prosperity, but when greater wealth leads people to have more comfortable homes, and then inevitably spend more time in them, there are laments about the increased atomisation of modern existence. Increasingly, people complain both about the hassle and expense of air travel and about the fact that the government isn't doing enough to combat climate change or to protect travellers from terrorism.

However, the answer, as usual, is not to stop complaining altogether. Such examples of wrong complaint can be made right ones by a few adjustments after some careful thought.

One option is simply to renounce one of the pairs of complaints as fundamentally misplaced. For instance, we might just accept that a more atomised, less cohesive society is the price we pay for greater freedom and prosperity.

However, the insight of pluralism is that, although we can't have everything, there is something of value in many of the things we do want. It may therefore be more sensible not entirely to renounce one in any given pair of contradictory complaints, and to see how we can make the competing claims between values into less of a zero-sum game and more of an opportunity for win-win.

To do this requires us to be more specific about what we are and are not complaining about. For example, if we lament the decline in traditional communities, we should not do so because we believe, all things considered, it is better for people to be born, live and die all in the same place. Rather, we might think that the decline in the shared life of a community has gone further than is necessary. We can't turn back the clock, but with better urban planning, local democracy and individual effort we may be able to make neighbourhoods more neighbourly. Similarly, it may well be the case that air travel should be more comfortable and pleasurable than it is, but that does not mean it should be cheap and frequent.

Such reframing of our contradictory complaints formally dissolves any actual inconsistency by accepting the impossibility of fully realising plural goods, while seeking to maximise the realisation of both. Hence we stop complaining about the decline of traditional communities and focus instead on the failure to develop a contemporary alternative. We stop complaining about individualism per se and think instead of how it may simply have gone a little too far. And we stop complaining about air travel as a single experience and instead pick on those aspects of it which really can be improved at no cost to the environment or to security.

Such an approach reflects two virtues of right complaint. One is *specificity*. The trouble with much complaining is that its targets are too broad. Such generalised moans are futile because they end up being directed at something that contains both good and bad, without disentangling them.

The second virtue is that of *proportionality*. Some of the most boorish complaints are wrong not in their content but in their extent. It is fair enough to complain about the failures of rail travel, for example, but not if you do so to the extent that you forget about the poor bus and coach users, let alone those sick or dying because of preventable diseases, war or famine.

If our complaints are both specific enough and proportionate to the seriousness of the failure of things to be how they ought to be, instances of contradictory complaint should be much rarer, if not entirely extinct.

Self-defeating complaints

Closely related to the category of contradictory complaints are self-defeating ones. These occur when we protest that things are not as they ought to be, but when the remedy would totally defeat the purpose of the complaint.

For instance, on arriving at the ruins of the Inca city of Macchu Picchu in Peru, you might marvel at it but also protest about how much better it would be if the crowds weren't so big. Yet if visitor numbers were strictly controlled, the chances are that you wouldn't be there to have the improved experience in the first place. Why would you think that you would fall into the, say, half of current visitors still able to get to the site, rather than the half denied the privilege? Unfortunately for anyone but a dictator, no one is ever going to pass a law which prevents *other people* from visiting places, but not *you*.

The complaint rarely seems self-defeating for us because we adopt all sorts of biases of thought which enable us to think restrictions wouldn't apply to us. We might believe that erecting obstacles would deter others but not ourselves, which would be to make unwarranted assumptions about the motivations of others. A wealthy tourist might assume that tighter rules would keep the smelly backpackers away, while the backpackers might assume that it would be coach parties who would be banned. Indeed, we could avoid being self-defeating by explicitly complaining in this way, but this would simply transform the protest into another form of wrong complaint, the self-serving kind (which I'll come to shortly).

In general, most complaints of the kind 'This is too popular' are self-defeating if taken as reflecting genuine beliefs that things are not as they ought to be, rather than as mere expressions of frustration. If it is hard to get a table at your favourite restaurant, that is probably because it is very good, and the only realistic way things would be easier for you would be if the restaurant lacked precisely the qualities that make you love it as you do. Complain if you will, but only as a form of catharsis.

Perhaps an even better example of a self-defeating complaint is the one often heard by advocates of diversity in culture. I'm a good (or bad) example of someone who likes to enjoy dabbling in cultural difference. As such a person, the heart always sinks a little if I go to a foreign city and find a Starbucks or Pizza Hut defiling an otherwise idlyllic scene of benign difference. If I were to complain about this, what would I really be saying? That cultures should retain their differences, and that we should not end up in a world where there is one big grey sludge of a monoculture, with nothing interesting and 'other' to embrace. But why would this be a good thing? Because that way people like me could enjoy the diversity.

But hang on a minute. The diverse world I want is one in which people like me could not easily thrive. I do not preserve any particular culture in its purity. My culture is a multi-culture, of curry one day, pasta the next, washed down with French wine, to a soundtrack of Brazilian bossa nova. If everyone were like me, everywhere would be culturally mongrel, and there would be no 'pure or 'authentic' national cuisine or music to dip into.

So it is clearly not true that I really want cultures to retain their purity, since to wish that would be to wish myself out of existence. What I really want, it seems, is for *other people* to be culturally monogamous so I can savour them with cosmopolitan promiscuity. It's like a libertine who wants his innumerable conquests to be chaste virgins. Once again, the only way to avoid my complaint being self-defeating is to make it self-serving.

Self-defeating complaints have something very important in common with contradictory ones. Both spring from a lack of acceptance of the limitations of life. In the case of contradictory complaints the problem is that of the plurality of goods.

This can also be the case with self-defeating ones. There are goods in both cultural purity and diversity, and having more of one can result in having less of the other. But self-defeating complaints can also spring from problems of accepting finitude. There are, for example, too many people chasing too few remote places. This is an unalterable fact. So if we do want to complain about there being too many visitors to such places, we need to do so in good faith, accepting the consequence that we ourselves should be able to experience less. The price we might have to pay for an unspoilt view of Macchu Pichu is that we never get to see the Galapagos Islands at all.

We find this hard to accept because, in the West, we have become experience junkies, reading lists in magazines and books of the hundred places we must visit or things we must do before we die and getting paranoid that we've only ticked off ten so far. Accepting we may have to settle for much less than everything is disquieting because it requires acknowledging how the finitude of our existence means many doors will never open for us.

Yet if we cannot accept this, we are doomed to utter more and more self-defeating complaints about how too many people want to do what we want, while failing to see that we are one of the people we are complaining about. Either that or our complaints lack any moral weight and become mere self-serving moans.

Self-serving complaints

I have a great deal of sympathy with anyone living near an airport who tries to halt its expansion. Trying to sleep under the flight path of a low-flying 747 is nobody's idea of fun. However,

I am very suspicious of any claims made on behalf of these local protesters (as opposed to peripatetic activists) that they spring from no more than a concern for justice and fairness. I am not aware of any research which would prove this, but I would be very surprised if the average protester against local airport expansion took fewer flights than someone of the same socio-economic group living somewhere completely different. Their concern is not with how airports interfere with sleep, but with how one *particular* airport may interfere with *their* sleep.

Fortunately, however, anti-airport protesters do not need to make their pursuit of self-interest naked, because there are now many environmentalist arguments doing the rounds which enable them to present their self-concern as concern for others. It may be true that the new runway will destroy sleep, but why rest my case on this if I can say instead that it will destroy the planet? If I am willing to fly from somewhere else, making such a green case would be profoundly dishonest. Honesty, however, is probably not the best policy, since though many may sympathise with your need for nocturnal rest, most will think a decent offer of compensation will more than make up for your loss.

Most anti-airport campaigns now run on a twin track. Green protesters take the moral high ground, arguing against all airport expansion, while other local residents argue for a more pragmatic case that further expansion is OK in principle but not here. Consistency is more readily available to the greens, just as long as they don't criss-cross the planet to make their protests, like the hundreds of people from all over the planet who descended on Puerto Alegre or Seattle to complain about globalisation, without any trace of irony. However, for the 'OK but not here brigade' double standards are hard to avoid, since everywhere is 'here' for someone.

Nevertheless, it is not difficult to find persuasive reasons why your area is the wrong one if you want to. For instance, as I write, Lydd airport in Kent is trying to get planning permission for expansion. Lydd is in one of the least built-up areas of the south-east and is close to the coast, and therefore expansion of flights there would probably cause less disruption to fewer people than probably any other airport proposal on the boards. Yet the Lydd Airport Action Group (LAAG) is not short of reasons why, actually, Lydd is a terrible place to expand air traffic. It cites factors such as 'serious public safety issues associated with locating a regional airport close to a nuclear power complex', a high 'risk of bird strike [...] as Lydd Airport is under one of the main migratory bird routes in the south of England' and threats to the jobs of 430 people who work in caravan/chalet parks on Romney Marsh. When it argues, however, that expansion would be better at the 'existing better-equipped Manston Airport', it is hard not to conclude that the main justification for this is the belief that expansion at Lydd would 'significantly reduce the quality of life of local residents'.[11]

Many, if not all, of LAAG's complaints therefore seem to be self-serving ones: complaints that seem to be based on justice but are in fact based on self-interest. This is the type of complaint most associated with 'Nimbys': protesters who say 'Not In My Back Yard'. Of course, no one is a self-confessed Nimby: the very idea reeks of hypocrisy. You can argue 'Not At All' on principle, but if your only objection is that it is close to you, the chances are you're guilty of supporting something as a social good which comes at a price, without wanting to be one of the people who pays that price. Any unpalatable side-effects must be somebody else's problem.

Of course, just as a stopped clock is right twice a day, so

it will be the case that sometimes, actually, Nimbys are right that their back yard is the wrong place. But like conspiracy theorists, the fact that a minority are right is no reason not to be suspicious of the majority who aren't.

The trouble with Nimbyism is not that it exists at all, but that it hides its own nature. As I said, I'd hate to have an airport expand near me, and if such a thing were proposed, I'd be entitled to say so. There is even a case for arguing that the decision should be made partly on the basis of who complains the loudest. For instance, the best argument LAAG has that Manston would be a better location is that the people there don't seem as bothered about it as Lydd's residents. The Manston Airport Group, for example, is explicitly not against expansion, it simply wants it to be done properly.

Yet Nimbys are rarely honest in this way. Or rather, they may be honest, but they act in bad faith, persuading even themselves that there are objective reasons to do with birds, rare frogs, jobs or whatever why their back yard really is the worst place in the country to build an airport, prison, recycling facility, wind farm or any other useful but unpleasant social utility. Such self-serving complaints are forms of wrong complaint not only because they dress up self-interest as justice but also because they manifest a self-interest which *believes itself* to be justice.

The call for a more honest Nimbyism, however, is likely to fail, because without the veneer of objective virtue, most such complaints fail to elicit any sympathy. Take the fuel protests of 2000 in the UK, for example. These were triggered by rising petrol costs, and the main focus of the protesters was the government's fuel price escalator. This was a policy of increasing duty on petrol above the rate of inflation as a means of reducing air pollution by encouraging more efficient use of energy.

This policy, with its clear social benefit for the vast majority, was eventually abandoned because of blockades organised by farmers and hauliers who felt the rising petrol costs were making UK trucks uncompetitive. The consequence of this volte-face, according to Cambridge Econometrics, was that by 2010 annual fuel use would be 11 per cent higher and carbon emissions 4 million tonnes greater than would otherwise have been the case.[12]

It is interesting in this instance how thin the protesters' argument really was. 'Parity with Europe' was the usual way of putting it: why should UK truckers and farmers pay more than their competitors on mainland Europe? Yet the protesters were not suggesting the solution was to raise fuel taxes over there, and hence get even greater environmental benefits. Equality merely provided an apparently fair justification for what was essentially an attempt to keep costs down. Nor is it at all convincing that rising costs threatened jobs overall: in the years after the protests fuel continued to rise in price on average faster than inflation, yet employment remained buoyant.

But then the veneer of justice did not need to be very thick, because most people drive and so aren't very keen on higher fuel prices. So it was that a great many people were able to convince themselves that their self-serving complaints were really something more noble. They were wrong, as many of us frequently are when we allow our self-interest to ally itself with a spurious, but apparently more ethical, aim.

Nostalgic and Luddite complaints

People always used to be so much better at complaining that nostalgia ain't what it used to be. The past so often seems better than the present. Woody Allen, in one of his stand-up skits, captures something of this in his tale of what happened when he faced hanging by a bunch of Klansmen. 'And suddenly my whole life passed before my eyes. I saw myself as a kid again, in Kansas, going to school, swimming at the swimming hole, and fishing, frying up a mess-o-catfish, going down to the general store, getting a piece of gingham for Emmy-Lou.' Yet here, as so often, the past is not quite as it seems. 'And I realise it's not my life. They're gonna hang me in two minutes, the wrong life is passing before my eyes.'

The problem is that when we recollect the past, it's very often a false life that passes before the mind's eye. Fings may not be wot they used to be, but they're not usually as we remember them to have been either.

Consider some of the things which are often said to have got worse in Western society over the years, such as diet. Today we are constantly told that we eat far too much processed, fatty and sugary food. It would be far better if we ate as our ancestors did, munching on wholesome food plucked straight from the garden or frying up a mess-o-catfish from pure, flowing rivers.

It's certainly true that the average Westerner's diet leaves a lot to be desired, but the idea that it was generally better in the past is surely delusional. Lack of fresh fruit and vegetables through the winter months meant that for much of human history northern Europeans were, by modern standards, mal-nourished for a large part of the year, if not the whole of it. In the 1930s the poor had what George Orwell called in *The Road to Wigan Pier* an 'appalling diet' based on 'white bread and margarine, corned beef, sugared tea and potatoes'. This was not just due to poverty. 'English people everywhere, so far as I know, refuse brown bread', wrote Orwell. 'They sometimes give the reason that brown bread is "dirty".'[13]

Even if we focus only on contemporary dietary crimes, I'm convinced they were much more prevalent in the 1970s, when I grew up, than they are now. Compare like for like, and today's consumers eat better on almost every count. Breakfast cereals were generally very sugary, such as Sugar Puffs or Frosties, or nutritionally thin, like Corn Flakes or Rice Krispies. Now, there are many more high-fibre cereals, and even the sweeter ones have had their salt and sugar levels reduced.

Then there is the bread, which if anything was worse than in Orwell's day. Sliced white 'plastic' bread, such as Mother's Pride, was all the rage, and wholemeal was still more or less unheard of in many households. Much bread continues to be terrible today, but at least more of it is wholegrain, while supermarket in-store bakeries have led to a revival in the consumption of fresh bread.

The range of fruit and vegetables available was very limited, and 'kiwi fruit' was still just a rude way of referring to a gay New Zealander. What's worse, many foodstuffs that had traditionally contained plenty of fruit and veg were being supplanted by synthetic, processed items. Knorr dried soup mixes were very popular but were little more than stock cubes to be dissolved into hot water and served as part of an apparently square meal. Fresh orange juice in the morning was still considered a bit of a luxury, and many preferred to buy Rise and Shine, a powdered orange-flavour drink. Even the perennial favourite the potato was getting short shrift, as the instant mashed potato Smash reached its peak of popularity.

The list could go on. It may well be true that where once schoolchildren were sent off with a small Penguin chocolate biscuit and a pack of crisps, they now also pack a larger Twix and a can of Coke. Not everything has got better since the '70s, but I would wager more is better than is worse.

Take the contemporary era as a whole, and it would be hard to argue that we would be better-off eating a pre-war diet. Despite all the gloom about how we're poisoning ourselves with junk food, we continue to live longer and healthier. Female life-expectancy in the UK rose by 3.6 years between 1981 and 2001, while males gained on average another 4.8 years of life. The number of years we could expect to live healthily also rose, less impressively, but still by more than two years for both sexes.[14]

Although we would surely be better-off if we ate less fast food, it is hard to justify the strength of feeling against it when you realise that this growth in life-expectancy mirrors the growth of McDonald's in the United Kingdom: in 1983 there were 100 branches of McDonald's in the UK, and by 2001 there were nearly 1,200. In other words, increased healthy life-expectancy is positively correlated with increased consumption of McDonald's food. Of course, it would be absurd to infer from this that eating more Big Macs is a cause of longer life, but it at least should make us question whether our diets were really better before fast food became a routine part of the mix.

If you are concerned about our eating habits, it is important that your complaints are not backward-looking ones, for the past should not provide the model for how we should eat in the future. Poor diet is an avoidable problem because we now have the resources to eat better than we do and did, not because we have lost touch with an older, better way of nourishing ourselves. We can enjoy greater variety of food with little environmental impact, owing to cheap and efficient shipping of foods from around the world. Technological advances have meant we can keep food fresher for longer without having to rely on dubious chemicals. We also know more about what really is good and bad for us, so we can rely on modern dietary science rather than old wives' tales to inform our eating. To complain that our current dietary problems are the result of losing touch with a mythical healthy past is nostalgic complaint of the worst kind, because by misidentifying the source of the problem it blinds us to the best, forward-looking solutions.

Nostalgic and Luddite impulses are often interpreted as being symptoms of neophobia, and hence wrong complaints that spring from them can be seen as reflecting a failure to see the opportunities offered by the new. However, I am not convinced that newness per se is usually the problem. The real cause is, I suggest, kainotophobia: fear of change. The difference between neophobia and kainotophobia is so subtle that you often see them defined as virtual synonyms, but I think the difference can be illustrated by the example of a typical pedlar of nostalgic whines.

Imagine a recently retired man, Ed. He will constantly tell you that life used to be better in the old days, but he is no neophobe. He lives in a new-build bungalow, drives a new car, has embraced the CD and the DVD, and uses a mobile phone. He is comfortable with anything new, just as long as it doesn't change his way of life in any fundamental way. What he doesn't like is that he no longer knows all his neighbours, that he feels unsafe walking the streets at night, that women are no longer 'ladylike', and that the kinds of jokes he likes telling are now 'politically incorrect'. The world he now lives in is not the world he knew and felt comfortable in, and, rather than change himself to fit the changing reality, he prefers simply to complain about how we're all going to hell in a handcart.

I've got a lot of sympathy for people like Ed. Maybe he really is too long in the tooth to change, and so he should carry on complaining as a form of catharsis. But although some of things he dislikes about modern life are regrettable, it would be undesirable to try to turn back the clock. The sense of safety and belonging he once felt cannot be replicated, because it has been undermined by greater social and geographical mobility, which is on the whole a good thing. Similarly, though it may be uncomfortable for Ed that women behave differently these days and that you can no longer crack jokes about 'Sambo', the gains for women and ethnic minorities that are linked to these far outweigh any loss to Ed and his ilk.

Not all change is for the better, and even good changes can have bad side-effects. But change is inevitable, and the old saying that we should try to guide change rather than stop it is no less true for being a cliché. Nostalgic and Luddite complaints are species of wrong complaint because they bolster a kainotophobia which stops us from adapting to and changing the transformations going on around us. We don't need to be neophiliacs to see this: novelty for its own sake is one of the shallowest of human pleasures. The right advice is 'Neither a neophobe nor a neophiliac be'. In the spirit of the serenity prayer we need the wisdom to see what is good in both the old and the new, and not to prefer one to the other merely because it is new or old.

Misdirected complaints

One of the main reasons why we abuse the noble practice of complaint is that constructive complaining is often so hard, whereas futile moaning is so easy. Most human beings are critical pessimists, always quick to see signs of fault and decline. It's not just that putting right all the ills of the world would take for ever: analysing all the ills correctly would take almost as long. Hence most of our complaints are issued prematurely, without sufficient thought, and, though provoked by genuine cases of things not being as they ought to be, they are fired off without any accuracy and either miss their targets or hit the wrong one.

Such misdirected complaints come in at least three forms: they can be *displaced, disproportionate* or *easy gestures*. The word 'displaced' is used here in its literal psychoanalytic sense. Displacement occurs when the mind redirects troubling emotions from a problematic object to something where the emotion can be handled more safely. This enables the potentially threatening nature of the emotion to be neutralised by finding an outlet in a safer form.

Psychoanalytic concepts such as 'displacement' are problematic to the extent that they give therapists power over their patients (as most still call their clients). An analyst may tell a man who devotes himself to the growing of asparagus that he does so merely because he is unable to confront the reality of his homosexual desires, and thus displaces his love on to phallic vegetables. If the gardener protests that this is nonsense, how are we to tell if it is the gardener or the therapist who is deluded?

Fortunately, however, we do not need to buy into the idea that analysts know our minds better than we do to see some merit in many of their conceptual tools. Where the analyst might see the strength of our denial that displacement is at work as an indicator of the likelihood of its reality, a more empirical reason for thinking there is something in the idea of displacement is that we can recognise when it is genuinely going on. Suggest to someone who really is focusing on work in order to avoid domestic problems that this is the case and, whether they admit it or not, they will probably be stung by the suggestion.

Displacement complaints are often the result not so much of denial as of following the path of least resistance. Consider the case of school dinners in England and Wales. The issue became a metaphorical hot potato after the celebrity chef Jamie Oliver made a television programme in which he revealed that most children were eating not much more than literal, fried ones. A generation was being raised on shaped and coated mechanically recovered animal matter with chips.

Oliver's exposé was genuinely shaming, but the reaction to it from a large part of the middle-class public was so strong that the suspicion was that the issue had become a lightning rod for something. Or perhaps some things: lightning struck more than once on this occasion.

The least edifying bolt came from a sector of the public which was basically disgusted by the working class. To put it crudely, many viewers found themselves thinking, 'No wonder they grow up to be fat, lazy, unemployed hooligans when they're raised on non-organic filth.' This claim may seem far-fetched, but in my experience a visceral abhorrence of the proletariat is remarkably common among the English middle classes. They happily use words like 'oiks' and 'chavs' to describe the poor, white working class, even though they would never dream of saying 'nigger' or 'coon'.

However, even these people know very well that it is not acceptable to despise someone on the basis of their social class or (lack of) education, and this distaste is something they don't merely try to disguise but wish they didn't actually feel. Hence if an opportunity arises to direct all that disgust, not at the poor little urchins themselves but at something else, why not take it?

Jamie Oliver's campaign provided just that outlet. All that disdain for the proletariat could be displaced on to school dinners, which could shoulder the majority of the blame for everything that is wrong with working-class life. Let them eat organic lemon polenta cake, and in the absence of chemical additives they will become less unruly, better able to concentrate, slimmer, more cultured creatures. The dividend is double: not only is the complainant absolved from any prejudice against the working people, but a socially unacceptable hatred is given an apparently moral outlet.

The furore was also the focus for a second displacement, almost a mirror image of the first. Here the displaced complaint was not against the horribleness of the working class but against the injustice of their plight. Despite over sixty years of the welfare state, with universal healthcare and education, life chances remain stubbornly dictated by accidents of birth.

Consider, for example, the depressing headings of a Power-Point presentation to the UK Prime Minister's Strategy Unit on life chances and social mobility by Stephen Aldridge, now its director: 'Those at the top and bottom of the income distribution are less likely to move between income groups than those in the middle'; 'People in unskilled or semi-skilled occupations are at much higher risk of unemployment than those in professional and managerial occupations;' 'Deprivation tends to be concentrated in certain geographical areas'; 'The infant mortality rate and the incidence of childhood mental illness are higher in unskilled and lower-income households'; 'There has been no narrowing of differences in life-expectancy by social class over the past thirty years'; 'Households on lower incomes are more likely to be victims of crime – and less able to protect their property from theft.' The litany goes on. What is shocking is that such findings are no longer shocking. We know that social inequality is stubbornly resistant to change by government policy, and few now believe we can do more than ameliorate it.[15]

To those who wish for a more equitable society it should be obvious that constructive complaint about inequality requires addressing issues of great complexity and intractability. This, however, is hard work, and aside from the plight of the less well-off, there are other problems that demand attention, such as choosing a new people-carrier, moving into the catchment area of a good school or cancelling the organic vegetable box delivery while the family decamps to a gîte.

Lucky, then, that something comes along which one can wholeheartedly support and which promises genuine changes in life chances for the poor. It turns out that we needn't worry about Marx's analysis of capital or Gordon Brown's harnessing of endogenous growth theory to fund redistribution: all we need to do is feed people properly. The poor needn't live on their knees; they can diet on their feet, standing taller than ever before, owing to stronger growth fuelled by five portions of fruit and vegetables a day.

The idea that better lunches can transform lives may seem extreme, but it's one Oliver overtly promoted. He made one family change what they gave their children for lunch and went back to discover that the kids' afternoon behaviour had been dramatically changed for the better. No one pointed out the obvious possibility that the presence of cameras, rather than vegetables, might have had something to do with this. Although there is indeed evidence that diet is important for concentration and energy levels, the idea that a square meal is a magic bullet for the ills of relative deprivation is absurd.

Such a solution appeals to the voice inside us that insists something *must* be done, even as another voice reminds us that not a great deal *can* be done. The complaint about the deep structural causes of social inequality can be displaced on to a complaint about school dinners, and thus instead of a painful, head-against-the-wall struggle we can focus our guilt on a single issue that can be solved by an education minister changing the menus. (Actually, the changes prompted by the programme had an unforeseen effect: the number of children taking school dinners went down by 20 per cent as they introduced healthier, but also less popular, menus.[16])

How many of the people who got excited over Jamie Oliver's quest for better nutrition were actually displacing complaints about the horridness or plight of the working class, I cannot honestly say. My point is to illustrate how displacement complaints can work, not to guess whether or not in this case they were at the heart of the phenomenon. What is surely true is that we are often tempted to complain about an issue which seems black and white rather than engage with an issue which is more complex. In a way, who can blame us? Life is hard, and expending endless energy on intractable problems is neither fun nor fruitful. But to displace our complaints is to avoid hard truths. You may prefer an easier life to a more honest one, but you should at least have enough honesty to recognise the fact.

It's not just supporters of Jamie Oliver's campaign who sometimes misdirect their complaints, however. So do those who criticise it. However, the fault here is one not of *displacement* but of *proportionality*. To protest too much about something that isn't very important can be an even more egregious example of wrong complaint than having a small moan about something you should be sanguine about.

In the UK some of the most informed criticism of Oliver has nonetheless fallen foul of this error. The entire healthy eating agenda has been rubbished by people who make too much of the kind of sceptical analysis of Oliver I outlined above. Despite the doubts, it is surely true that it is preferable that schools feed children better, not worse, and that we eat well. There may be too much emphasis put on this, but in reacting against it we have to be careful not to overcompensate. Being lectured by a politician on how many vegetables I should be eating a day may make me want to go out and devour a box of Krispy Kreme doughnuts, but I would be foolish to interpret this desire as an act of rational resistance against the hegemonic oppression of a paternalist state.

Once again, complaints against Oliver were disproportionate. Oliver was just one man doing his best to help the kids and raise his ratings (there is no contradiction between the two). Even if his programme was symptomatic of a wrong turn we have taken in the UK on health and diet, in itself it was largely benign and possibly even beneficial. To complain too much about it is to get things out of proportion, even if there is some substance to the complaint.

Such disproportionate complaints matter because they divert finite energy towards the wrong ends. It is not just that there are more important issues than children's right to eat Turkey Twizzlers. It's also that if you want to counter the excessive rigidity and zeal of nutritional advice, you shouldn't pick on the one target who may actually have a point.

Perhaps even worse is that people are repelled by over-the-top complainants. As an atheist, I face this problem with my more militant peers, who are so vociferously against religion that people who might otherwise be sympathetic to secular humanism end up being put off. Richard Dawkins is the most famous example of this, although, as a matter of fact, in the substance of what he says he tends to be much more thoughtful and careful than his public image suggests. But people do judge books by their covers, and Dawkins presents his anti-theistic arguments in very strident, confrontational terms. His best-selling book was called *The God Delusion* and his television series *The Root of All Evil* (a title which he now says he regrets).

If there's a queue to complain about the falsity and perniciousness of religion, I'm in it with Dawkins. But if, when my turn comes, I make it sound as though religion is nothing but a delusion and lies at the root of all evil, I think I'd be guilty of getting things out of proportion. And so I would have lost the chance to persuade some people who might otherwise see the light (or perhaps I should say, turn it off).

Not only can complaints be misdirected by being disproportionate or displaced; they can also be both. The clearest example of this is what might be termed environmental anality. I have to confess to being prone to this myself. After a train journey I will take my newspaper and empty plastic bottle home to be recycled, even though when I see the sackloads of trash being offloaded at the terminus I have to accept my meagre effort is a droplet of mist in a vast ocean.

Making this extra effort oneself is, at worst, harmless. What is worse is to complain about other people's tiny wastes of energy and resources. It is true that if 'everyone did their bit' together we would make a difference, but this is irrelevant because everybody is not going to do it unless they are forced to. Recycling rates in the UK shot up only because local councils were set targets and so acted to make people separate their trash. In a similar way, the kinds of mass waste of energy stand-by buttons represent is going to be avoided only when manufacturers are forced to stop putting them on appliances; and aviation growth is not going to be significantly halted by a few idealistic people taking their holidays in Lyme Regis instead.

So when we complain about relatively small wastes of energy, we are guilty of both displacement and lack of proportionality. We haven't got things in perspective, because throwing a newspaper into a bin is too small an act to make any difference to the environment. But we're also displacing, because the scale at which these problems have to be tackled is too large for us to have any direct impact on it. Rather than feel helpless, we will go into psychological distortions to convince ourselves that every little really does help, rather than facing the reality that our personal actions are as useless as collecting our sweat to help put out a forest fire.

This doesn't mean 'going green' is pointless. We should do our bit, mainly because we should practise ourselves what we preach for all others. It's just that, when it comes to complaint, we should focus on changing policy, not the habits of friends and neighbours.

Green politics, however, is a fertile breeding ground for a third kind of misdirected complaint: the grand but empty gesture. Such complaints tend to occur when people are looking for an opportunity to make a stand. Primed with this incentive to find something to complain about, and do it loudly, they often end up choosing not on the basis of sound facts and good reason but on what would make the biggest splash.

The case in 1995 of the Brent Spar oil storage buoy in the North Sea off Scotland is a good example of this. When the Brent Spar came to the end of its working life, its owner, Shell, needed to dispose of it. It basically had two options: bring it to shore for dismantling or dump it deep out at sea in the Atlantic. Shell undertook its own study of the two options and decided that deep-sea disposal was the safest option, both because it posed a lesser risk of industrial accident and harm to its workforce, and because it would have less impact on the environment. In particular, there was a risk of its breaking up in shallower waters as it was brought to shore, which would have had a greater impact of marine life than sinking it in deep sea.

For Greenpeace this was an opportunity to make a big public stand against dumping at sea, which it opposed in all circumstances. It sprang into action, with activists occupying the platform and testing the levels of pollutants on board. Greenpeace's media campaign was highly successful. Most of the public agreed that the platform should not be dumped in deep sea, some boycotted Shell petrol pumps, and the share price of the company fell. Shell eventually bowed to public pressure and abandoned its plans, even though it insisted that these had represented the safest option and the company still had the backing of the UK government.

What is dispiriting about all this is that Shell was probably right, and Greenpeace later had to apologise for grossly overestimating the levels of pollutants on the buoy. Fortunately, nothing did go wrong when the Brent Spar was brought to land for dismantling, but the fact that a risky decision comes off does not mean the risk was worth taking in the first place: I would be a fool to claim that surviving a game of Russian roulette vindicates my decision to play it.

For Greenpeace the complaint did fit its wider purposes, since its campaign was fundamentally based on opposition to dumping at sea, not on any specific claims about the relative merits of doing so on this occasion. Although it may seem bizarre for a green group to care less about the actual environmental impact of a decision than about broader, long-term goals, it is not inconsistent.

More guilty are the ordinary people who were too quick to back Greenpeace and dismiss Shell's claims as smokescreens for profiteering. Without checking the facts, millions leaped to make a gesture on behalf of the environment and against big business by backing Greenpeace and shunning Shell. The opportunity arose for an empty gesture, and too many took it.

The similarities with other variants of misdirected complaint are clear, most notably the preference for the easy, quick hit over the harder, more considered option. It's just easier to fire complaints at a clear, big target than it is to wade through the facts and complications to reach a more considered view. Misdirected complaints are above all a testament to our laziness, our longing for the simple black and white in a world of bewildering grey.

Paranoid complaints

There is an old wisecrack that goes, 'Just because you're paranoid, that doesn't mean they're not out to get you.' Like many of the best jokes, however, it has an element of truth, and not just in the obvious point that not everyone who feels persecuted is imagining it. More interestingly, most instances of what we might call non-clinical paranoia build on a vast mass of truth.

Non-clinical paranoia is not a mental illness, though the obsession it often fosters can eventually lead people to the sanatorium. It is, rather, a cooler version of the false belief that there are unrecognised or unacknowledged forces operating against the individual or society. In contrast to the clinical paranoiac, who simply imagines things that are not there, the non-clinical variant makes understandable errors of reasoning.

The world is full of non-clinical paranoiacs, who can be identified by their tendency to make what could be called second-order complaints. At the first level there is the basic complaint (9/11 was a CIA plot, the BBC is run by leftists, Jews fix US foreign policy etc.); but then at the second level is the complaint shared by all of them: that this terrible truth is being somehow suppressed. To put it in the formulation I have used to define complaint, not enough people know that things are not as they ought to be, because things are not as they ought to be at the level of knowledge transfer either.

Such thinking can be seen as paranoid because of how these two levels of complaint fit together. In order to believe both that things are wrong and that this fact is not acknowledged as the simple truth that it is, it becomes necessary to ascribe to people who have an interest in suppressing the fact incredible powers of knowledge management. For if this weren't the case, why on earth wouldn't more people see the truth for what it is? Hence the postulating of the suppressing, powerful agent behind the scenes becomes essential to maintain the coherence of holding a truth that so few are willing to accept.

Non-clinical paranoia is widespread because it is so hard to hit the 'Aristotelian' mean when it comes to credulity. Aristotle persuasively argued that right ways of thinking and conduct tended to fall between two extremes. Courage, for example, lies between the excess of rashness and the deficiency of cowardice. Generosity avoids the excess of profligacy and also the deficiency of meanness.

We don't always have words to describe the mean or its two errant neighbours. Complaint is a good example. A person who complains too much is a moaning minnie or a whinging fool; a person who doesn't complain enough is a doormat or a pushover. But we lack a word or phrase for the person who complains just enough and in the right way. I might suggest we refer to such a person as a quintessentially Aristotelian complainant, but for the fact that it is a horrible mouthful and the obvious acronym would make such a person a 'quac'.

Credulity is another axis of virtue which lacks a suitable word for the mean. Those who accept what they are told too readily are called credulous or gullible; those who go to the other extreme are over-suspicious, cynical or non-clinically paranoid. Those in the middle can be described as persons who proportion belief to evidence and argument in the appropriate way – which, again, is hardly a phrase that's usable in everyday speech.

As is so often the case, these two vices are not accorded the same degree of seriousness, and how they are viewed varies tremendously according to what social circles you move in. In many intellectual circles, for instance, it is de rigueur to be utterly sceptical about everything that Western politicians do. This is particularly true of people who adhere to what might be called Cod Chomskyism, or its British counterpart, Knee-jerk Pilgerism. Neither of these creeds should be confused with exactly what Noam Chomsky and John Pilger actually say and write. They refer, rather, to a broad set of background assumptions which inform the political analyses of generally middle-class chatterati who pride themselves on how they are able to see through the charade of official political discourse.

Put simply, this world view is based on two claims which are assumed to be true unless proven otherwise. First, the USA acts internationally with the sole motivation of furthering the financial interests of American capitalists in general and the interests of the military–industrial complex in particular. Second, the USA furthers these interests by making sure its allies, client states and any other nation it has some leverage over follow its will.

Everything else follows a priori from these two claims. So,

for example, what if the White House is headed by a president who does not share these goals? It doesn't matter: the power behind the throne is what counts. How does one decide whether to back the USA or its enemies in any given conflict? That's easy: never back America. Because its motivations are never benign, you can be sure you've backed the right horse if you side against it, even if the enemy appears to be evil. After all, labelling anyone who stands in the way of US hegemony 'evil' is a tactic favoured by the powers that be to create a moral smokescreen for their selfish intent. The enemy of my enemy (the USA) may not quite be my friend, but he should certainly be granted a benefit of the doubt not accorded to America. Given that the USA is often criticised for being too quick to side with the enemy of its enemy, this is especially ironic.

This may look like a gross caricature: surely no one could buy into such a one-dimensional, simplistic view of international relations? But the frightening thing is that if you take this account to be true, it passes one of the key tests of a scientific theory: predictive power.

Consider, for example, Tony Benn's farcical interview with Saddam Hussein in 2003.[17] Benn had travelled to Baghdad, as he put it, 'to see whether, in a talk, we can explore, or you can help me to see, what the paths to peace may be'.

How would someone who buys into the cod Chomskyian analysis of global conflict approach such a serious task? Well clearly they would assume that any reasons offered by the USA in favour of military intervention were baseless shams, and one would then be as charitable with America's enemies as you were uncharitable with the USA itself. Of course, that is exactly what Benn did. When Saddam said 'Every fair-minded person knows that when Iraqi officials say something, they are trustworthy', he didn't object at all, even though if President Bush had said something similar about the American government, he would have laughed him out of court. Nor did he flinch when Saddam blamed sanctions, not his own manipulation of them, for the deaths of Iraqi people, because it is obvious that if blame could fall on America or its enemy, it should fall on America.

To say this is not to defend the policy of the USA in Iraq but simply to point out the absurd one-sidedness of an analysis which ends up portraying a mass-murderer and tyrant as a poor, oppressed foreign leader, the innocent victim of neo-colonial bullying.

The same kind of convoluted thinking is found in Pilger's own Chomsky-inspired analysis of NATO's campaign in Kosovo in 1999. Whatever you make of the double standards employed by the USA in its foreign policy, explaining why it should get involved in a local conflict far from its shores, with little or no strategic importance for itself, for reasons which fit the cod Chomskyian–Pilgerist picture, would seem to be pretty difficult. This is especially so in this case, because the campaign was fought by NATO, which meant persuading various other states to take part.

Difficult, yes, but not impossible. In an article on the conflict in 1999, Pilger claimed that stimulating the arms trade was the real reason for the war. In particular, '[the] terror bombing of Serbia and Kosovo provides a valuable laboratory for the Anglo-American arms business'.[18] Amazingly, all the other NATO member states were somehow hoodwinked into committing their soldiers to fight a war solely to help the US and British military–industrial complex. After all, NATO is now simply 'an instrument of American global control'.

You could not wish for a clearer example of non-clinical paranoia. First, there is the *prima facie* plausible complaint:

the USA is a global bully which never acts ethically. Then you have the problem that its actions in Kosovo don't seem to fit this mould. No problem, in comes the second-level thinking: the reasons are there, it's just that the USA is so good at hiding its intentions and getting other people to bend to its will that it can get all its Western allies to take part in a war that doesn't benefit them at all. You are thus forced by the logic of your own position to end up with a hypothesis of a state which has incredible power and control over foreign governments.

Once you start down this road, there is no going back. For example, there would appear to be a huge contradiction here: despite its supposedly enormous power, the US government has clearly not been in control in Iraq, or even back at home, where it failed to deal properly with the aftermath of Hurricane Katrina – politically and practically – and George W. Bush's approval ratings went into free fall. But facts can always be made to fit the theory: you just need to claim that any *apparent* lack of control is all part of the plan. Disorder in Iraq is not incompetence: it's strategic neglect.

You can see how this leads us to the mark of paranoid thinking: nothing can count as negative evidence. If Iraq is brought under control, the USA is getting its way; if it is not, it is still getting its way, because it wants the country to be a mess. If the USA intervenes in foreign states, that is neo-imperialism; if it doesn't, it's evidence that it lacks the moral commitment to end the suffering of a people. If it tried to intervene against every tyrannical regime, it would be a hubristic bully; if it goes into Kosovo and Iraq but not Zimbabwe or Darfur, it's inconsistent and hypocritical.

The US government seems to attract more paranoid complaints than most, and there is a good reason for this, which takes us back to the problem of following the Aristotelian mean for credulity. The truths that fuel the paranoia are that the USA is the most powerful state in the world, that people do lobby it to pursue their own narrow interests, and that politicians are not incorruptible. Therefore an attitude of suspicion is entirely fitting. Indeed, it is surely worse to err on the side of gullibility than on the side of cynicism. But where it all goes too far is where, in order to sustain the coherence of the primary complaint of abuse of power, a second-order complaint has to be invoked that ascribes to hidden forces a power that the evidence suggests no government has ever had.

Woody Allen sends up the absurdity of this in *Annie Hall*, when Allison, an exasperated girlfriend of the protagonist, Alvy, sums up just who exactly would have to be in on the conspiracy, if the Warren Commission was fixed, namely 'the FBI, and the CIA, and J. Edgar Hoover and oil companies and the Pentagon and the men's room attendant at the White House'. 'I would leave out the men's room attendant', says Alvy, almost biting the whole bullet. (The pay-off is perhaps even more truthful. Allison says, 'You're using this conspiracy theory as an excuse to avoid sex with me', and Alvy replies, 'Oh my God! She's right!')

I'm not saying that all the non-clinically paranoid are sublimating their sexual desires into totalising theories of mass deception, but having such an all-encompassing theory of why things are both wrong and prevented from being known as wrong certainly gives you a false sense of being in on something important. Such complaints can take over your life, for, if right, they are clearly more important than almost anything else we have to deal with.

Which takes us back to the joke about how paranoiacs may nevertheless sometimes be right. A rather different film, *Independence Day*, makes good sport with this idea. A raving

conspiracy theorist is talking about the famous Roswell incid-
ent, in which it is claimed a UFO was captured and taken to
the secretive Area 51, where it has been kept ever since. The
president of the USA tells him, 'Regardless of what the tabloids
have said, there were never any space craft recovered by the
government. Take my word for it, there is no Area 51 and no
recovered space ship.' At which point his chief-of-staff clears
his throat and says, 'Uh, excuse me, Mr President, but that's
not entirely accurate.'

One of these days what I have called a paranoid complainant is going to turn out to be right. To hit the Aristotelian mean
on credulity we have to be careful not to dismiss all apparently
outlandish claims as outrageous. However, unless we recognise the perverse logic of paranoid complaints, we're not going
to be able to distinguish the apparently implausible from the
merely extraordinary.

Conformist complaints

Of all the things that are not as they should be, other people
surely come top of the list. The list of complaints we have
about 'people today' is endless: they watch too much television, especially reality shows; they are unable to appreciate
orchestral music and just listen to bite-sized chunks on com-
mercial radio stations, or buy compilations as background
mood music; they eat rubbish; everyone is just out for themselves and doesn't care about society any more; attention spans
have reduced to virtually nothing; we take our democratic
freedoms for granted; and so on and on and on.

I have to admit some of those criticisms sound plausible
to me. But I'm suspicious of them because so often I think the

real complaint is simply that 'people are not like me'. Accepting that people are different seems to be so hard: we much prefer to believe they are inferior.

Music is perhaps the prime example of this. It seems that we cannot drop the habit, acquired in the playground, of judging people according to their musical taste. Virtually everyone feels an involuntary, strong desire to say that the music they despise is really, factually, not very good, rather than just not their cup of tea. Take Dick, who works in the record store in the film *High Fidelity*. When a customer asks him if he's got 'I Just Called To Say I Love You', he refuses to sell it to him because 'it's sentimental, tacky crap'. Abominable though his behaviour is, like many who saw the film, I was instinctively on his side. The thought that someone who likes Stevie Wonder's worst three minutes must be defective in some way is irrepressible. This is despite the fact that there are no reasonable criteria of what makes some music better than others, nor any evidence that musical taste is a marker of good moral character.

Lovers of classical music in particular seem prone to snobbish judgements on the basis of musical taste. Their prima facie justification for this is that their favoured music is more complex, nuanced and sophisticated than mere pop or rock. It obviously takes a more refined sensibility to appreciate Mahler or Beethoven, because it takes time and careful listening to even be able to appreciate it properly. In contrast, the simple tunes and rhythms of hip beat combos popular with the kids are like Blue Nun compared with Château Lafite. So it is that the connoisseurs of high music do not just observe the fact that others do not appreciate it: they believe that such unappreciative souls should know better, and at least ought not to go crazy for the aural bubblegum they do listen to.

Such complaints have no basis. It is bad enough that

classical music lovers disagree fervently among themselves as to what is truly great or not: Tchaikovsky even called Brahms talentless. Far worse is the fact that there are numerous factors we can cite when judging music to be good or bad, and no style has a monopoly over them.

Take, for instance, the case of funk. To the classical music buff funk is music at its most brain-dead. It is repetitive, melodically simplistic and usually verbally crass. Yet great funk can be all those things, and none the worse for it. The whole point about funk is that it is based on the rhythm section, building on looping bass lines. The great innovation of funk, as made by its leading practitioner, James Brown, was a simple rhythmic one: the beat fell 'on the one' – the first beat of the bar, not the second. The change was a genuine innovation, no less so for being so basic.

What makes a great funk track is that it builds up a good groove. Even here, though, there is room for great musicianship. Not many musicians can be as 'tight' as James Brown's greatest backing band, the JBs, who hit every note and beat at just the right time, with the right emphasis. (If they didn't, Brown would dock their wages.) Funk sounds free and rambling, but to play it well you need tremendous control.

Even the lyrical simplicity is part and parcel of the joy of funk. For a singer like James Brown, words – as well as grunts, moans, shrieks and screams – are essentially sung for their percussive quality. If you try to read the words of '(Get up I feel Like Being a) Sex Machine' as poetry, you really are missing the point.

Today, of course, there are serious musicologists who will vindicate funk's worth by describing it in similar terms. But its quality is proven before the analysis: music is first judged to be worth listening to, and then people describe what makes it notable. When it comes to that first judgement, there is no objective way of saying whether it is right or wrong.

It might be argued, in reply, that although no one genre is objectively better than any other, it is still the case that some examples of that genre are better than others. So, for example, pop is no better or worse than Baroque chamber music, but the Beatles are better than the Cheeky Girls. When we complain that people listen to rubbish, we are therefore legitimately saying that they ought to be listening to one kind of music rather than others.

This argument may be one way of saving a kind of objectivity for judgements about musical taste, but it does not vindicate the complaint that people ought not to listen to inferior artistes, because it does not imply that people ought to take their music more seriously. I am very tempted to accept that if you really like soul, for example, you'd be better-off listening to Isaac Hayes or Marvyn Gaye than you would the latest ersatz product of a TV talent show. But what I can't defend is the view that you are wrong if you don't make the effort to seek out these better practitioners of the art. If you're satisfied by listening to second-grade soul in the background, then there is no particular reason why you should sit down with a copy of *What's Going On?* and see how it really should be done. The complaint that people ought to take their music more seriously is no more justified than the complaint that they listen to the wrong kind of music. The rational case for both has been definitively shattered by the stark empirical fact that all sorts of nasty, immoral human beings have been musical connoisseurs.

All sorts of other complaints about how people are today are likewise unjustified complaints that they are not as we would like them to be, for no better reason than that their tastes and preferences are not ones we feel able to embrace. People who watch television are looked down on by people who read books, even though many TV shows are more enriching than most contemporary fiction. Liking burgers and fries is likely to get you looked down on, but since when has culinary taste been a marker of moral or intellectual character? Most ridiculously, we often tend to think people ought to take more interest in what we ourselves think important: philosophers decry the lack of philosophy in the culture; historians the decline of interest in history; economists the naïvety of politics not steeped in economic theory; and so on. From the inside it really seems to these people that their specialist subject is more important, but if you take a more objective view, the only way to sum this systematic bias towards one's own area of expertise is with the absurd injunction: people ought to take more interest in what I am interested in. This is the brute desire for people to conform to your own conception of the good life, disguised as moral outrage. And when you broaden out the frame of reference from my personal preferences to those of my social group, you get snobbery: other people should be like our people.

The irony is that received wisdom says that we all now believe in 'each to his own', and that the problem of contemporary society is supposedly that we've gone too far in embracing a laissez-faire relativism. I think this is often just skin-deep. When it comes to the crunch, we often have a remarkably fixed and narrow idea about how people should live. In general terms we are all pro-difference. Get down to specifics, and toleration is often as far as we can go, and our disapproval can't wait to find an outlet in the form of a complaint about how the way people live today really is appalling.

Empty complaints

There is one final category of wrong complaint which is simple to identify but hard to avoid: complaining about things that just aren't the case. A trivial but telling example of this is of the UK restaurant chain PizzaExpress. In the late 1990s and early 2000s it became a common complaint that their pizzas were not as large as they used to be. However, this was just not true. It was simply the case that more competitors had sprung up, and their pizzas were bigger.

Eventually, in 2002 the company bowed to the inevitable and added 50 per cent to the area of their pizza bases. Although they explicitly denied having previously shrunk them, for many this was the smoking gun. Even today people will swear blind that they know for a fact they had indeed got smaller. We trust our memories, even though psychologists have proved that our recall is far less accurate than we think it is.

This is a sobering example of how, when it comes to a battle between objective fact and subjective perception, the truth rarely wins. Once we get a fixed idea in our heads about the way things are, we start processing the data from our senses in a different way, placing too much emphasis on that which confirms our perception and disregarding that which denies it. Psychologists call it 'confirmation bias', and it is very hard to avoid.

When you write for newspapers and magazines, you get used to people complaining about things you simply have not said, and attributing motivations to you that they lack any evidence for. If, for example, I criticise something Michael Moore has said, I get accused of a right-wing bias, even though the week before I was having a go at George W. Bush. Criticism of Noam Chomsky is even more likely to get you black-listed by his many acolytes, who seem determined to prove the accusation of paranoia with their disproportionate indignation at any negative representation of their hero. In a mirror image of Bush logic, it seems that you are either for Chomsky or you are for state terror. (It is a further irony that Chomsky writes about how the powers that be manufacture consent, yet many Chomskyites brook no dissent.)

We make too many assumptions on the basis of too little information, and although I am sure this is a universal human flaw, Freud has not helped us here. In albeit bastardised forms many ideas that emerged in Freud have got a grip on the Western imagination and have become truths universally acknowledged outside psychoanalysis, even if they are false.

One of the most pernicious such ideas relates to the Freudian slip. While it is no doubt true that unintentional gaffes and malapropisms can reveal the actual state of our minds, we have tended to take this too far, so that we now trust too much in the power of tell-tale small signs to reveal what we really think.

A good example of the consequences of this overconfidence concerns the inferences that practitioners of Neuro-Linguistic Programming (NLP) claim they can make about a person on a basis of their eye movements. This is not the place to discuss whether these claims are valid or not: the theory is, at the very least, controversial. What interests me more is how well disposed people are to accept that the NLP model is right. It now seems like perfect common sense to believe that unintentional movements will expose the real self within, so when someone comes along with a particular example of how this works, people readily believe it. Instead of saying, 'That sounds like a rather big claim: can you substantiate it?', too many simply say 'Is that so? How fascinating!'

Our overconfidence in our ability to judge people on the

basis of tell-tale giveaways has been made worse by the cod-psychoanalytic way of thinking which so many of us have adopted. This leads us to make complaints on the basis of little more than our own biased perception.

How well are you able to control this reflex? Here's a little test. Below are ten complaints which I suspect many readers will be tempted to make on the basis of what they have read so far.

1. You say that the Bible is read by believers as literal truth.
2. Christianity *has* often encouraged people to complain against worldly injustice, as has Buddhism.
3. Positive thinking can be very useful.
4. Contrary to your claims, there are sound reasons for favouring many pro-environment measures.
5. If we followed your advice, we would ignore anti-airport protests, because they are simply rooted in selfishness.
6. Diet *is* an important public health issue.
7. You're an apologist for American neo-cons.
8. You have denied that there are any meaningful ways of making aesthetic judgements.
9. You have dismissed NLP without evidence.
10. You accuse Noam Chomsky, a far greater intellect than you, of paranoia.

None of them, however, accurately describes what I have actually said. Such complaints would be empty because they are directed at things that just aren't there. Yet I know from experience that many will make these and similar complaints nonetheless, because they trust in their ability to glean, from the examples I use and the targets I hold up, the real truth about what lies behind my arguments.

That's why, although I have detailed several varieties of wrong complaint here, the most efficient way of reducing the number of wrong complaints you make is simple: just check whether what you are complaining about is actually the case. If everyone followed this simple injunction, I predict that the background noise of pointless complaint would almost disappear, and we would then either focus on the complaints that really count, enjoy life a bit more, or perhaps a bit of both.

4

QUOTIDIAN COMPLAINT

There's an old Jewish joke about two women having lunch in a restaurant. 'I don't know why we come here, the food here is lousy', says one, to which the other replies, 'Yes, and the portions are so small.' Jokes about complaining are not rare. The 'waiter, waiter' joke is an entire genre based on complaints, but the set-up is just an excuse for some absurdism and wordplay: we're not laughing at things that we actually complain about. Even the joke about the people in the restaurant turns on the ridiculousness of the way we sometimes complain, not a serious complaint in itself.

In order to be funny, joking about the things we complain about has to avoid getting too close to the things which really make us angry. The limiting case of this is found in much contemporary stand-up comedy. This often touches on serious issues that really do bother people. For example, in one of his routines Chris Tucker was going through a skit in which he imagined Michael Jackson as a pimp, and the mainly black audience was screaming with laughter. Then he segued into more serious territory. 'White people don't trust black people.' Laughter still, but less raucous, as though Tucker was still riding the wave of his previous tour de force. 'That's why they won't vote for no black president.' The audience is almost silent. 'Like, a black brother will fuck up the White House.' A few chuckles. Tucker is talking about something that generates serious complaints and it's just not funny.

However, he soon gets laughs from the idea, but only by taking us back away from the unpleasant reality to the realms of the absurd. 'Like the grass won't be cut', he continues. The loud laughter is back, and so is the applause. The crazy list goes on: 'Dishes piled up … basketball in the hallway … broken down cars on the driveway.' He's back with what's funny, and though it is rooted in a serious complaint, it can't be too close to it, because the things that we really think are not how they ought to be just aren't funny.

Slavoj Žižek illustrates this point very powerfully with his observations about humour based on ethnic stereotypes in the former Yugoslavia. 'There were obscene, vulgar jokes about how each nation was identified in Yugoslavia with a certain characteristic', he says. 'We Slovenes were misers, the Croats nationalists, the Bosnians sexually obsessed but stupid, Montenegrins lazy, Macedonians thieves.' Žižek's claim is that this showed, not that people really hated each other, but that they were comfortable enough with their differences to joke about them. 'My ultimate negative proof', he says, 'is that with the rise of true tensions in the early '80s, these jokes disappeared. This was the best signal that something was really wrong.'[19] Jokes may have the surface appearance of a genuine complaint, but when we're really bothered by something, we can't laugh about it.

So most of the comedy of complaint is concerned with exaggerations or caricatures of serious complaints, such as Turner's riff on how white people don't trust black people, or complaints we don't actually care too much about. Consider, for example, the endless comedy routines about the differences between men and women. These are based on such witty 'observations' as the fact that women take a long time to get ready to go out, that male genitalia are ugly, that men don't like asking strangers for help and so on. If any of these things really, deeply annoyed you, you wouldn't laugh at them.

(In a similar way, we may laugh at what we fear, as Freud suggested, but the joke can't simply be the presentation of what is truly terrifying.) That's why it's depressing to be a feminist at a comedy club when everyone finds the 'observation' that men will fuck anything that moves absolutely hilarious. The fact that most people are in stitches shows that they don't really mind the things the comic is ostensibly complaining about. More than this, the routines provide a kind of affirmation: 'Yes, this is normal, aren't we funny with our foibles!' It's also the reassurance that 'men are men and women are women'.

The popularity of such routines illustrates the fact that although, at its noblest, complaining is one of the most important things we can do, most of the time it's not much more than a leisure activity. We like complaining. Indeed, sometimes it's hard to avoid the conclusion that we actively seek safe things to complain about. I had a wonderful example of this in the form of an appreciative email about a newspaper article I had written, which began 'Once again you stop my daily rant at *The Guardian* in its tracks ...' I've had a few others that say similar things, which invites the question, why read *The Guardian* every day if you know that reading its contents is going to irritate you?

This kind of relationship with news media seems to be very widespread. I noticed it in myself when I started to keep a diary, cataloguing all the complaints I made, heard and read. My little list was greatly extended by an hour with the Sunday paper. I complained about the infantilisation of the paper; about comments by Norman Mailer, reported on the occasion of his death; about the filling of pages with things which just weren't news, about the rehashing of old stories as though they were new; and about the smug superiority of the film reviewer. It seemed that part of the ritual of reading the paper was to moan about it, just as for many people watching television becomes primarily an opportunity to lament the poor choice of programmes available.

I was a little embarrassed to discover just how much I was complaining. We may all believe that 'everyone likes a good moan', but it's a generalisation we apply more readily to others than to ourselves. Or so I thought: I now suspect that being seen as someone who doesn't complain is judged by most people to be as undesirable as being perceived as someone who complains too much. This hypothesis emerged from the experience of running an online survey, as I was writing this book. Nine hundred and twenty people took part, answering questions about how much they thought others in their country complained, and about how much they thought they complained themselves. The list of complaints they were asked to rate for frequency and intensity were very ordinary, quotidian complaints, the kind you hear in pubs, on trains, in homes and offices every day: about the cost of living, politicians, public transport, how things have generally got worse, bad luck and so on.

At the end of the survey each participant's result would be compared to those of others. Those *kvetchers* in the top ten percentile of complainers earned the label *über-complainer* (*Homo querulus maximus*); the above average mere *complainer* (*Homo querulus*); the average *Goldilocks complainer* (*Homo pondera*); the below-average *patient type* (*Homo patiens*); and the bottom 10 per cent *Zen doormat* (*Homo placidus*). As the monikers emphasised, these were not to be taken too seriously (so please don't get upset if the Latin is wrong). Nevertheless, self-assessment tests like these exert a strange power over people. The results seem to take on a kind of bogus objectivity.

I thought that the people who would contact me to say that my categorisations were wrong would be those who came out as *über-complainers*. In fact, this is not what happened, partly perhaps because anyone would see the self-defeating nature of writing to complain that you have been falsely labelled a complainer. Instead, a fair number of people told me that they thought the test had *underestimated* the extent to which they complained. 'I do complain quite a lot, but not about the things you listed', the protest would run.

This surprised me, since I had assumed people would prefer to be seen as non-complainers. Perhaps this response was merely a by-product of the category names: 'Zen doormat' implies an excessive passivity. However, another feature of the results makes me suspect that this is not the whole explanation. The results enabled me to compare how much people thought others complained about thirteen different things with how much they thought they themselves did. Again I had assumed that people would think others complained more than they did, and I still suspect that if you asked the simple question 'Do you think you complain more, less or about the same as other people?' more would answer 'the same or less' than 'the same or more'. But my survey did not ask for an overall impression; it actually got people to focus on particular types of complaint. The result was that people thought that they complained significantly more than they thought others did. Expressed as a percentage, where 0 per cent would represent no one ever more than rarely complaining about anything, and 100 per cent everyone regularly complaining about everything, the average 'complaint factor' scorer for how we perceived others was 48 per cent, whereas it was 64 per cent for ourselves. For every complaint bar one, on average, people thought they complained about it more than others did.

The exception to this rule was religious leaders: for some reason people have the perception that others complain about them more than they themselves do. This was true in both the USA and the UK. I'm not sure why this would be so, except for the fact that the 'new atheists' – such as Richard Dawkins, Sam Harris and Christopher Hitchens – have got so much attention in recent years that people perhaps have the false sense that religion is more under fire than it is. Since religions thrive on persecution, they themselves have a stake in buying into this impression. My survey suggests, however, that this perception is false.

I want to stress that the nature of my survey means that its results have to be treated with extreme caution. (See the appendix for more about this.) But even if the reality is not quite as it seems, combined with my other observations, at the very least it suggests to me that people have some sense that to be fully human is to complain. No one wants to be seen as a moaning minnie, but even worse is to be seen as someone who doesn't complain enough.

However, as I have suggested earlier, it does seem that we expend too much energy complaining about the wrong things. The highest rating subject of complaint, for ourselves and others, was 'bad luck or fate', which scored 85 per cent and 71 per cent respectively. But this is an example of the most basic kind of wrong complaint: one directed at something that simply cannot be changed. At best, such complaints are cathartic; at worst, they divert our energies from things which we could actually do something about.

In contrast, the least complained about, again for how we perceive ourselves and others, were ineffective politicians (30 per cent and 48 per cent). Interestingly, 'corrupt politicians' scored more highly (43 per cent and 59 per cent). This seems odd to me: I would rather politicians were effective but a little corrupt than ineffective but blameless. It is true that corruption can make politicians much less effective, as has sadly been so often the case in Africa, but that is beside the point: if effectiveness is what we want, then corruption at the scale which would interfere with this is automatically ruled out.

Also low down the scale of things we complain about were two things we can do something about: poor service (51 per cent) and bad-quality goods (59 per cent). It seems very odd that we complain more about things totally out of our control, such as the weather (68 per cent), the cost of living (60 per cent) and how things have generally got worse (73 per cent). Of course, the fact that these things are beyond our control is what makes them more frustrating, but it does not make them worthwhile objects of complaint, save as catharsis.

But I don't think this entirely explains our propensity to complain about things we know we cannot change. It also seems that complaining is a kind of leisure activity. We often complain because we enjoy it: if to complain is to be human, then it reaffirms the fact that we are alive and still sensitive to the myriad ways in which life is not as it ought to be. A man who is tired of complaining is tired of life.

And there is so much that is not how it ought to be. When I kept my complaint diary, I found that on the whole the complaints I heard concerned the small irritations of everyday life. For instance, taking a train, the first complaint came from the ticket seller, whom I had asked for a complicated combination of tickets in order to avoid paying the standard full fare for my route. He lamented the passing of the supersaver ticket class and the general rise in prices. Once on the train, someone had to complain, very politely, that someone else was in their seat. Others complained about problems they'd had with their reservations, while others talked about non-communication in their office.

A particularly interesting couple were on their way to a meeting of the Fellowship of Reconciliation, a Christian non-violence group. They were pretty good grumblers, lamenting, among other things, the fact that one of the fellowship's campaigns was called 'Living by the Sword' and that the person collecting rubbish on the train was not separating the different items for recycling, as well as expressing some dissatisfaction with who was either already on the committee or up for election to it. What they never once complained about was violence in the world.

What I think this shows is how even those who embrace the nobility of complaint cannot give up its more frivolous variants. Even when we're on our way to discuss matters of life and death, the pull of trivial, quotidian complaints is as strong as ever. This is partly because the truly important things that are wrong with the world weigh too heavily for us to shoulder them all the time, and partly because we can't seem to switch off the sensor which alerts us to what is wrong all around us. And why should we? Human beings did not get where they are today by being sanguine about imperfection. The meek would have no world to inherit if the more petulant did not set about building one fit to last.

Understanding the nature of everyday complaint helps provide a counterweight to the more lofty ideals of complaining that I have been advocating. It is true that we spend too much time complaining about the wrong things, wasting our most human and divine of capacities. But it is also true that there is plenty of complaining to go around, and we should not get too puritanical about purging complaints which are pointless from a utilitarian point of view. Complaining is a social activity, something we enjoy for reasons I only partly understand. It's a capacity we feel almost compelled to exercise, which is perhaps also one reason why complaint can feel cathartic. Since there is only so much of real substance that we have the energy for, most of the time we're doing the complaining equivalent of working out, keeping in shape for the times when it really does matter. Recovering the nobler nature of complaint requires not abandoning its more mundane varieties but simply getting them in proportion.

Comparative complaintology

So far I have talked about complaint as a human universal. But isn't it likely that there are differences between what different groups of people complain about and how they do it? I think that's almost certainly true, and the main purpose of my survey was to try to find some clues as to what these might be.

I say 'clues' because I do not pretend that my survey was scientifically rigorous enough to provide anything like a definitive verdict. But there are reasons for taking seriously what it shows about *variation* in answers depending on country of residence, gender and age. Even if the total sample set is skewed in some way (which it almost certainly is), differences within this set which hinge solely on one of these factors probably are indicative of some more general trends.

NATION

Most respondents to the survey came from the USA and the UK, and their answers point to some intriguing similarities and differences. Americans and Britons were strikingly alike in one respect: their overall levels of self-reported complaining were very close indeed, with their complaint factors varying by only 2 per cent, which statistically speaking is as good as identical. Given that there were other real differences between the two nations, this may lend more credence to the view that, although what we complain about and how we do it may vary, the need to complain in some way is a constant.

One trivial factoid from the survey is that, contrary to stereotypes, the British complained less about the weather and public transport than the Americans, both relative to other complaints and in absolute terms. A more significant difference was the gap between how much people think they themselves complain and how much they think others do. In both countries people judged others to complain less than themselves, but that gap was 4 per cent larger in the UK than it was in the USA. This may reflect the persistence of the ideal of the 'stiff upper lip'. It is still seen as not terribly British to complain too much, and hence Britons tend to assume that their fellow countrymen are a less grumbly lot than they really are.

However, the truth that underlies this perception may be that Britons really are less likely to express their grievances in public. This interpretation is reinforced by a question in which respondents were asked to choose which of two statements they thought more accurately described their country: 'people tend to complain to others if they are not happy' or 'people tend to keep their complaints to themselves'. In both Britain and America most thought people were more inclined to voice their complaints, but this was much more marked in the USA, where 10 per cent thought their compatriots kept quiet about their protests, as opposed to 29 per cent in the UK. Similarly, twice as many Americans as Britons agreed that 'People tend to complain to the people responsible for their grievance', rather than that 'people tend to complain among their friends, but not to the people with power to change things'.

I think that this reflects one of the biggest cultural gaps spanning the Atlantic. Put simply, America has an optimistic culture, Britain a pessimistic one. The distinction is not as boldly binary as this, but the difference in emphasis is, I think, quite clear. Complaint is a revealing lens with which to look at this distinction, since it starts with the observation that things are not as they ought to be. Given that, what happens next? An optimist thinks that they can be better, a pessimist that we're stuck with the imperfection. This is what the survey results suggest about the USA and the UK: Americans complain because they want and hope things can be better; Britons complain largely for the hell of it. Americans believe in the perfectibility of the world and look confidently towards the future; Britons have an Eeyorish sense of life's grimness and a conservative attachment to the way things are, no matter how flawed.

The survey again backs this up: the British complained more than the Americans about 'how things have generally got worse', both in absolute terms and in comparison with the other complaints they could rate. But the main evidence for this interpretation comes not from my little survey, but from what we can see for ourselves in American and British life and culture. For example, time and again American foreign policy has been based on the hope of spreading freedom and democracy around the world. Sceptics say that this is never more than a rhetorical cover for the real intention, which is to promote American interests. I think that to take either view as the whole truth would be naïve: motives are almost always mixed, and I think US foreign policy makes more sense if you assume both sets of considerations (and others) have a part to play.

However, this kind of Utopian belief in a free world strikes the British as frankly barmy. Many Americans may find this hard to believe, but when Britons hear US presidents talking about spreading freedom and justice, most of them just laugh. To the British it seems fake, so they're very ready to believe that it really is fake. But this betrays a lack of imagination and understanding of America's past. American optimism seems unreal only because the British have become so cynical they could never imagine anyone saying this sort of thing with sincerity.

These differences were played out in the build-up to the second Iraq war. Americans seemed more willing to believe that the liberation of Iraq would be welcomed with open arms by the Iraqi people, and that bringing democracy to the Middle East would be, if not easy, the most probable outcome. Selling the war in Britain on these lines, however, was never going to work. Britons were impressed by the moral imperative to remove a nasty dictator but were even more impressed by the idea that, if we didn't, Saddam would pose a real threat to national security.

These differences were reflected in the speeches made by George Bush and Tony Blair as war got closer. On 23 February 2003 Bush made his vision of post-Saddam Iraq central to his speech. 'The nation of Iraq, with its proud heritage, abundant resources and skilled and educated people, is fully capable of moving toward democracy and living in freedom', he said.[20] Two days later Blair addressed the British parliament and talked almost exclusively about disarming Saddam, removing the threat he posed and enforcing UN resolutions.[21] Making regime change a primary objective was politically unacceptable in the UK. For the British, polls showed that the invasion was initially supported by a small majority (no matter what impression was given by the famous mass marches barely a month earlier), but only as a dirty job that had to be done. America, it seems, genuinely had higher hopes than this.

The role of Tony Blair in all this is also instructive. He was often portrayed as Bush's poodle, an impression bolstered by the famous 'Yo, Blair!' video, which showed him weakly trying to offer his help to a visibly nonplussed George W. Bush. But the facts show that Blair described Saddam as 'probably the most dangerous ruler at the present time anywhere in the world' and claimed he was trying to develop weapons of mass destruction even before his first meeting with Bush.[22] Blair's apparent distance from the British people and closeness to America was largely a result of his belief in the possibility of building a better world, which was alien to most of his fellow countrymen but very familiar to Americans.

The old and new countries can learn from each other in this respect. The apparent pessimism of the British is in many cases no more than a hard realism. But the can-do attitude of the Americans is not always excessive optimism. The Brits should learn that the point of complaint can and should often be actually to change things; Americans that you can complain all you want, but some things can't be put right.

The most extreme variation between the two countries, however, concerned perceptions of politeness. Whereas Britons were split 50–50 on whether or not their compatriots tried to be polite when they complained, an overwhelming majority of Americans (85 per cent) chose the other option available, that they tended to show their anger or irritation. This was a massive difference. Since different cultures have different baselines for what behaviour is considered rude or polite, could this just be a result of different expectations? Probably not, because respondents would still have answered relative to these baselines.

In any case, we don't need to rely on the results of the survey, since observation backs up the numbers. Americans are much more direct in their complaints than the British, who are still learning that it's OK to complain in the first place. However, it is not simply a matter of directness: if even Americans think that people complain rudely, then there is more to it than just an absence of obfuscation.

I suspect that the difference has to do with entitlement. America is a much more profoundly individualistic culture than the UK. I'm not talking here of the individualism which rejects community. Indeed if anything, outside the big cities, Americans appear to be more community-minded than the British. American individualism is deeper than this, in that everything is based on the sovereignty of the individual over herself, her property and her possessions. This means that, if you pay for something, you're entitled to get exactly what you expected. The burden of proof lies with the government to justify its taxes, not with you to say why they shouldn't take them. However, this does not mean Americans are selfish: there is a greater expectancy in the USA than in the UK that people should do voluntary work and make charitable donations.

The British, in contrast, have a more communitarian outlook. Certainly, the mythology of Britain says that it is the 'mother of the free'. But in practice Brits tacitly accept that the general will has some authority over them. They grumble about taxation but do not see it as the great evil in the way Americans do. They also put up with bad service because they do not make the simple inference that, since they've paid for it, they are entitled to demand it as a right. There are several reasons why this may be the case. There is the old deference to authority, which demands that we should be grateful to our betters for what they deign to give us. This has weakened, but its decline was matched by the growth of the welfare state, in which many services were either paid for, or subsidised by, general taxation. This made the link between what we pay and what we get much less transparent and thus made people feel less like consumers and more like grateful recipients of state beneficence.

Translated into the manner of complaint, it is clear why Americans should demand what they see as rightfully theirs without standing on ceremony and why the British should be slightly apologetic about pointing out that things are not quite ideal. We are often told that things are changing and that Britain is becoming more of a service culture, like America. But as is so often the case, the existence of a trend is too often misinterpreted as a sign that we are closer to where that trend is leading than we really are. If Britain is a chaste maid to America's strumpet, she has barely learned to loosen her corset.

GENDER

There are probably more preconceptions about the importance of gender for complaint than there are for any other demographic indicator. However, the striking thing about my survey was how comparatively slight the differences between the sexes was. Nor can this be easily dismissed as an artefact of the survey design, since other variables, such as nationality, did reveal large differences.

The overall levels of self-reported complaint were more or less identical for the two genders, a finding that fits those of one of the few psychologists to do serious work on complaining, Robin M. Kowalski.[23] It could be argued that this is uninteresting, because people determine what they perceive as complaining a lot or a little by different yardsticks. So the almost identical results would show that the sexes complain equally only relative to the norms for their respective genders. If these norms were different – if men complained much more than women, for example – then the survey results wouldn't reveal this.

However, we have a check against this theory: people's perceptions of how others complain. Again the sexes are more or less in agreement here, with men estimating the amount others complain slightly higher than women. But if it is the case that the two sexes more or less agree about how much people in general complain, then their assessments of how they themselves complain are being measured against the same yardstick.

The only explanation that remains which is consistent with actual differences between the sexes is that either men or women are more accurate or honest about assessing how much they complain. If this were the case, then both stereotypes and psychological research would lead you to expect that women would be the more accurate judgers, since their 'emotional intelligence' is reputedly higher than that of men. But the small difference that there was in the survey actually showed men thinking they complained more than women. Differences in degrees of self-knowledge do not therefore seem to explain similarities in reported levels of complaint.

So although the survey is itself not a rigorous piece of evidence, it does strongly suggest that men and women complain more or less equally. But are there any differences in patterns of complaint? Again, not very many, and these were much less marked than those between nationalities. If you looked at the complaint factors for British men, British women, American men and American women, the scores closest to that of any given group were not generally those which shared gender. So, for example, British men's scores were closest to those of British women five times, American women four times, and American men a further four times. More often than not, the complaint factors for British women were closest to that of British men rather than American women (or men). All this suggests that nurture may often be more important than nurture in fashioning our patterns of complaint: our biology may have less effect than our culture on how we complain. The only two forms of complaint where gender was much more important than nationality were those about spouses, partners and friends, and those about personal ill health. These are both things which men were much more likely to complain about than women. If any propensity to complain is determined by gender, it is likely to be these. If this could be confirmed, it would raise a number of important questions about why it is that married women, in particular, are more likely to be called nags than their husbands. Despite advances made in the cause of female emancipation, it does seem still to be the case that society is less tolerant of complaining women than it is of complaining men.

Setting aside nationality and looking at where the difference in levels of self-reported complaint were most marked, women complained more than men about ineffective politicians (8 per cent difference), television (10 per cent) and religious leaders (13 per cent). This defies the stereotype that the big issues of politics and religion are the domain of men. Feminists may not be surprised by these results, however: the hierarchies of most religions are solidly male, and women have less representation in almost all (if not all) governments than men. No surprise, then, that they might feel annoyed about being messed about by a load of men. As to why they should complain more about television, perhaps the tendency of the major channels to devote huge amounts of prime time to sports played by men and watched mainly by them has something to do with it.

The only other significant result concerning gender related to perceptions of whether people complain to others when they are not happy or keep their complaints to themselves: 11 per cent more women than men thought that people complained to others. Perhaps this is a case of automorphism: projecting characteristics of ourselves on to others. The question's inclusion of the phrase 'if they are not happy' suggested a strong emotional component, and men almost certainly are, on average, less inclined to talk about problematic emotions than women. From this they are therefore more likely to generalise that this is what is normal for others.

However, the main conclusion from the survey is one not of difference but of sameness. Perhaps this does support one of my main claims: that the desire to complain is an essential part of human nature. If this is so, unless you thought women were less human than men, or vice versa, you would expect both sexes to complain about as much as each other, even if about slightly different things.

AGE

As might be expected, overall levels of complaint rose with age, by a steady 1 per cent each decade. But this is a very gentle statistical incline indeed, which does not point to major differ-ences in average rates of complaining across the generations.

More surprising was that people claimed to complain *less* about how things have generally got worse as they grow older. These complaints peaked in people's thirties (78 per cent), but even twenty-somethings thought things had got worse more than the over-forties, with the over-sixties least inclined (67 per cent) to protest that things aren't what they used to be.

Of course, because this is all based on self-reporting, it is possible that people are just wrong about this. But remem-ber that, in general, people rated their own levels of com-plaint *higher* than those of others. This gives us some reason to believe that people are not in denial about how much they protest themselves and have a reasonable grasp of their own tendency to complain.

On reflection, it would perhaps not be surprising if it is indeed the case that Luddism peaks in people's thirties. At this stage in life many are still coming to terms with the loss of youth. In many ways things really were better not so long ago: you had fewer responsibilities, more energy, and the world was newer and more exciting than it has now turned out to be. Furthermore, you have not really seen that much change: there is only now and the last few decades.

Once you are older, however, it becomes less easy to make blanket generalisations about the superiority of the past. In the UK, for example, people over forty remember periods in the nation's history when life was quite evidently worse in many ways. Standards of living are much improved from those in the post-war decades, while more people now enjoy better cars, foreign holidays and better, more varied food. Also, older people have seen more change and thus are no longer compar-ing just the imperfect present with one, romanticised, past.

It may still be the case that older people make more specific complaints about how particular things were better in the past: the question in my survey was about whether life has *generally* got worse. Anecdotally, this would seem to be the case. Older people are often not shy about telling you how the streets used to be safe and there was more respect when they were young. Overall, however, fewer say that they'd rather live as they did back then than the way they do now.

Not that old age seems to give people the wisdom and tranquillity to accept life's vicissitudes more easily. The over-sixties complained more about bad luck or fate than any other age group: a staggering 90 per cent of them claimed to complain about it regularly. The image of the elderly curmudgeon is also somewhat supported by the fact that complaints about spouses, partners and friends rise steadily with age, dropping off only slightly in the over-sixties, who have perhaps lost too many to maintain their earlier levels of cynicism.

The stereotype that age jades was borne out in other ways too. People were less inclined to complain about religious leaders and politicians as they got older: more, I'd guess, because they see no point, rather than because they grow to respect them. The idealism of youth turns into either a realism or cynicism of age, depending on how you view it.

Complaints relate more to practical things of individual concern: public transport, which older people tend to rely on more; personal ill health; the weather; and the cost of living, which becomes more of a factor, as income is usually much lower after retirement than it is in peak earning years.

There is something dispiriting in the fact that complaint about the big issues of public life, such as politics and religion, is largely the preserve of youth. It is perfectly rational that, as we age, we come to see the futility of much raging against the machine. Our mistake is to let this become too much of a habit, so that a justified cynicism about the possibility of change makes us too weary to act when it really could count. The benefit of age and experience should make us better equipped to fight the battles that can be won and really do matter. Right complaint should combine the engagement of youth with things of real importance and the wisdom of old age to see what can actually be changed.

Towards a future complaintology

If my survey results are no more than suggestive, then at least I hope they show that there are serious issues which could be raised by a more systematic and rigorous study of patterns of complaint. The few sociologists and psychologists I could track down who had done substantive work on complaint both reported that little other work on it had been done in their respective fields.

This is a pity. That this is not at all a trivial subject can de demonstrated by considering what it might mean if the broadest summary of my survey were corroborated: that people generally complain more or less equally, irrespective of culture, gender or age, but that what precisely they choose to complain about can be revealing about their values and beliefs. The first part of the conclusion points to the existence of that rare and endangered species: a human universal. Against the tides of cultural relativism few truly transnational human traits remain standing, and those that do tend to be the most basic: eating, working, copulating, forming groups and creating rituals. Complaining belongs on this list, not as a curiosity but as a reflection of our possessing both a moral sense and the spirit to talk, and act, on the basis of it.

The variety in what people choose to complain about, however, is potentially even more interesting. If it is indeed true that culture affects complaint behaviour more than gender, for example, this would feed into the often frenzied and muddled debates about nature and nurture. What it suggests is that, although there are real differences in the underlying psychologies of men and women, reflected in their complaint patterns, it would be a mistake to focus too much on these, since most of these differences pale into insignificance when compared to cultural ones. If you want to know why someone complains comparatively little about poor service, for example, the answer is in the passport, not the chromosomes. And if this is true, then the extent to which such sex differences as there are reflect nature or nurture is highly questionable.

The psychology and sociology of complaint therefore feed into its politics. I argued earlier that complaint is at the root of all social change. But who gets the opportunity to complain the loudest? Whose complaints are heard without prejudice, and whose are dismissed? These questions are important, for they have a direct bearing on how much power different social groups have to reshape the world into a more just and equitable form. Once again, complaint is shown to be no trivial matter, but an issue which is at the heart of who we are as social animals.

5

COMPLAINT AND GRIEVANCE

In the USA recently I caught sight of a large billboard by the side of the highway. It looked like an advertisement for a TV crime drama or a film: a couple of smart-suited guys stood confidently, superimposed against the backdrop of a nocturnal cityscape. In fact, what this slick, stylish ad proclaimed was 'We Sue Drunk Drivers'.

Litigation has been big business in the USA for many decades now, and there are signs that the UK and Europe are following suit. In recent years there has been an increase in British lawyers seeking damages for clients on a 'no win, no fee' basis. Advertising campaigns now ask people if they have had an accident and whether someone could be to blame. If you answer yes, then the promise is that a big cheque could be yours.

This trend is much lamented. Robert Hughes's *Culture of Complaint* was one of the first serious attempts to critique the book's eponymous phenomenon.[24] That every page contained some kind of complaint by the author was ironic but not damning: right complaint *should* drive out wrong complaint. Ever since, people have been queuing up to complain about the complainers. Their argument is that we have developed a grievance culture, in which we routinely try to deal with our misfortunes by seeking legal redress.

Although I agree that we do live in a grievance culture, I think its nature is not properly understood. To see what lies behind it, we need to look at social changes coalescing around three key concepts: responsibility, freedom and entitlement.

Responsibility

It is often claimed that the grievance culture stops people from taking responsibility for their own actions. Accidents are no longer things that just happen: they are opportunities to pin the blame on someone else and make yourself a fortune. However, it is not just that we are given an incentive to shift the blame to others; we are almost forced to do so, because in a grievance culture, if you can't blame someone else, someone else will probably blame you.

You see this at work in the advice given to motorists by insurers, never to accept responsibility in the event of an accident. People are not merely choosing to deny their responsibility, they are being obliged to do so by the people with whom they enter into legal contracts. This can require us to deny what we know obviously to be true. For example, when I wedged the bumper of the car in front of me into its rear left tyre, I knew it was my fault for not keeping my distance and braking too late. Why on earth should I deny a self-evident truth? But this is what happens when the idea of responsibility ceases to be a moral notion and becomes a legal one. One pins blame and denies responsibility for legal reasons, and the question of who was morally responsible is irrelevant. From a moral point of view, for instance, it is insane to suggest that a café's owners have to make sure you don't burn yourself on the coffee they serve. But since Liebeck *v.* McDonald's in 1994 – when the fast-food chain was successfully sued by a woman who burned herself on a take-out coffee she had placed between her knees – the legal precedent has been set, and the moral argument is swept away.

The overturning of morality by law is the recurrent pattern of the grievance culture. There are several different social and historical factors which are all working to push us in this direction, as the possibility for genuinely moral interaction with our fellow citizens diminishes.

Actual morality, as opposed to theoretical ethics, has generally had two rather different pillars: the institutional and the social. The key institutions of morality have been religious authorities, which have set out the moral law for laypeople to follow. However, the extent to which these edicts have really shaped behaviour is debatable. For sure, many sexual mores, for example, have been fashioned by the Church. But in the quotidian interaction of people social constraints probably have had more force than theological ones. When we lived in small towns and villages, the knowledge that we would see the same people again and again acted as a natural moderator of our more selfish impulses. Many of the moral injunctions that guide us on a daily basis are necessitated by the practical needs of living in close proximity with others. For example, life becomes very difficult in a small community if you get a reputation as a liar, so truth-telling becomes a practical as well as a moral imperative.

Both these pillars have come tumbling down in modern urban and suburban life. Most people no longer recognise an ecclesiastical authority as a source of moral rules. When the most Catholic country in Europe, Italy, has one of its lowest birth-rates, you know that the authority bishops command over their flocks is very weak indeed. Nor can we rely on everyday social life to provide our moral compass: when so many of us don't even know our neighbours, the kind of moral self-regulation small communities evolve is also dying out.

Social conservatives say that the result is a crisis of moral legitimacy. They are right, but what is striking is that this has not yet translated into a crisis of moral behaviour. People are floundering around without any clear sense of what grounds their values or constrains their actions, but this has not led to the decline of Western civilisation. Indeed, on many counts, the decline of moral certainty has positively correlated with great moral progress. People today are much less tolerant of spousal abuse, sexism, racism, ageism, ableism, drunk driving, violence against children, rape and exploitation of workers in the developing world: and the list could go on.

The crisis so far has largely been manifest in a confusion about what justifies and grounds ethical values. In terms of how we actually live, I see little sign of moral disaster. But, of course, that doesn't mean we should assume this will continue. If our ethics lacks an understood and agreed basis, it is vulnerable to challenges from alternative moral systems, amoralism or, as has already happened, legalism.

The priority of law over ethics is thus an understandable development. Law gives us a framework to order our behaviour which promises to combine the objectivity of religious codes with the rationality of modern thought. It also deals with the problem that we can no longer use daily interaction with neighbours to nurture our sense of moral propriety. For example, in the UK neighbours have frequently been in dispute in recent years over the height of Leylandii hedges. Since neighbours don't know each other as they used to, and may not even be able to presume they share each other's core moral commitments, the possibility of resolving these disputes through reasonable dialogue has diminished. Into this void steps the law, so that you can take the matter to your local authority for them to sort out. Instead of relying on neighbours to behave well towards each other, we now rely on rules to determine what we can or cannot do.

Making the concept of legal responsibility central to our

ideas of right and wrong enables us to avoid worrying about our moral responsibility. This kicks in at two levels. First, we become less inclined to worry about whether something is morally right just as long as it is legal. The distinction between tax evasion and tax avoidance is instructive here. Tax evasion is illegal, but tax avoidance uses legal mechanisms. Most people would be delighted to be told by their accountant that they can avoid tax by exploiting some kind of legal loophole. Anyone who felt uneasy about following such a course of action would probably be told that there is no need to, because what they are doing is totally legal. However, taxation is also a moral issue, based on the Marx-lite principle that each contributes to the common purse according, roughly at least, to ability. If you support the moral case for taxation, it is hard to see why finding a legal way to avoid paying your share is something you should feel smug about. But as our norms become more and more guided by law and less by an autonomous ethics, we see less and less reason to take anything into account other than an act's legality.

The second level of loss of responsibility concerns our choice of moral values themselves. Jean-Paul Sartre argued that we cannot avoid being responsible for the values we choose. Even if we simply follow rules set out by priests, we still have to take responsibility for choosing those priests as moral authorities in the first place. However, Sartre argued that we do not like to admit this to ourselves or others, because the responsibility would weigh too heavily on us. Hence we prefer to kid ourselves that deferring to the authority of others transfers our responsibility over to them.

Sartre would recognise straight away a key psychological motive for the drift from ethics to law: while it is hard to deny that we choose our own values, we are genuinely not responsible for most of the laws which we are obliged to follow. We choose our legislators only in a very indirect way, and most people at any given time have not voted for the government in power. So if laws provide the normative underpinning of our behaviour, we can truly achieve the kind of escape from responsibility Sartre claimed we craved.

Seen in this light, the relationship of cause and effect between the rise of grievance culture and the decreased willingness to take personal responsibility for our actions is more complicated than it may at first seem. The increased legalisation of normative discourse has occurred in large part because the moral discourse has become so enfeebled. Once this trend reaches a critical tipping point, it becomes self-reinforcing, since the de facto precedence of the legal becomes a cause as well as an effect of the decline of the moral. Simply to blame the increase of litigation for the waning of morality is to put the cart before the horse.

The moral-to-legal shift also explains the diminished moral status of complaint. A more legalistic public discourse encourages more vocal and strident complaint, since if you do have a bona fide legal complaint, you are in the legal right and there is no arguing against you. There is thus an objectivity to legal complaints which brokers no dispute, in contrast to moral complaints, which always have to be argued for and can never be adjudicated with any finality. For that reason, if you are seeking resolution to a grievance, it is far better to make a legal complaint than a moral one.

This obviously means that, over time, we hear more and more legal complaints and fewer and fewer moral ones. This in itself diminishes the sense that complaint is a moral act. What's worse, the complaints we do hear no longer have any basis in morality, only in law. And finally, because such complaints are so often about individuals or groups seeking redress for their own problems, complaint becomes associated with self-serving pleading, not a cry for an end to general injustice.

The sense in which a grievance culture is one where responsibility is diminished is therefore much more profound than is usually thought. We are encouraged to complain more and more, but without a moral basis. Moral responsibility is undermined because morality itself is undermined, replaced with a straightforward, unambiguous but ethically shallow legalism.

Freedom

Where do you hear most the complaint that our hard-won freedoms are under attack? In countries that are the most free, of course. This is not illogical: the more freedoms you have, the more you have to lose, and the more opportunities people who don't like your freedom have to try to remove them. However, this does have the somewhat perverse result that the freer people are, the more problematic that freedom appears to be.

The argument that our legalistic grievance culture is one of the most pernicious current threats to freedom follows from the concerns about responsibility. Because people are less willing to take personal responsibility, they are also less willing to take personal risks. The connection is twofold. First, the grievance culture fosters an intolerance of failure. When bad things happen, the first thought is that someone must be held to account, and legal, or quasi-legal, mechanisms must be brought into action to do so. In such a climate the baseline assumption is that someone, somewhere, is underwriting the risk for you. It is simply intolerable to accept that that something could go wrong without recourse.

One well-documented consequence of this is what is known as moral hazard. This is where people modify their behaviour and take more risks because they feel that they are not fully responsible for the consequences. For example, people may worry less about household security if they are confident that their insurance will cover any losses. Similarly, tourists may take valuable equipment into situations where there is a high risk of loss or theft, if they know that their travel insurance will cover them.

However, less discussed is the risk-*reducing* effect of the grievance culture. Although we may become more willing to take risks that are underwritten in some way, we are less willing to do things that are not. The presence of some kind of insurance is not an extra reassurance, it is the norm, and so to do something in the absence of guarantees becomes reckless.

One example is travel insurance. People used to travel abroad routinely without any cover. Most did so without any problems, but the few who hit difficulties paid a high price. Travel insurance has helped those few, but it has now become so routine that to travel without it seems dangerously rash. What was once an extra level of security now becomes a minimum requirement and is indeed often a contractual obligation when you book a holiday. Yet is it really a risk worth worrying about, for example, to travel without insurance as an EU citizen within the European Union, where reciprocal agreements between governments ensure that you are covered for emergency health problems anyway? I don't think so, but it is surprising how many people feel exposed if they arrive at the airport realising that they have no insurance cover.

This has a negative effect on freedom because it turns us

into risk-averse self-constrainers. Sometimes it is others limiting our freedom, such as companies who require that you get insurance before they take your custom. But more often it is ourselves who step back from doing things which we fear are not adequately covered. The whole notion that life is naturally fraught with risk is undermined in a culture that holds all risks are ultimately the legal responsibility of someone else.

The second link between the grievance culture and freedom is that the fear of litigation limits what people are prepared or able to do. There are many stories, for example, of schools organising fewer trips and extra-curricular activities because they are afraid they could be sued if anything goes wrong. One British teaching union, the NASUWT, recently went so far as to advise its members against taking part in outdoor activities because of the risk of litigation in the event of an accident occurring. As Michael Power put it in his pamphlet *The Risk Management of Everything*, we are becoming not so much risk-averse as responsibility-averse.[25] The fear of being held responsible for something going wrong makes us unwilling to take any risks, with the consequence that we are less and less free to do what we want.

These two links reinforce each other and end up severely limiting what we are willing or able to do. We want others to carry the can for anything that might go wrong, but others are understandably reluctant to take on the responsibility. Our two fears are equal and opposite forces that leave us paralysed, unable to do what either party wants. Schools and parents both want school outings, for example, but each party wants the other to shoulder the responsibility for failure.

There is a great political irony here. Traditionally it has been the political right which has criticised the 'nanny state' for limiting our freedoms, and indeed it is often still the right which complains about the culture of litigation. Yet this grievance culture is rooted not in state paternalism but in the privatisation of responsibility. Private solicitors acting on behalf of private individuals are suing private (and public) bodies, within the framework of civil law. The root of the problem is the unfettered pursuit by individuals of their own personal interests. Where the statist left arguably reduced people's sense of personal responsibility, the grievance culture exaggerates the sense we have of other people's individual responsibility. Between left and right, an appropriate sense of our own limited but real responsibility has been squeezed out.

Yet without an appropriate sense of responsibility and its limits we can have no true freedom. Freedom and responsibility are intimately linked. We do not give freedom to people such as young children, who are not able to take responsibility, nor can we truly grasp our own freedom unless we are able to take responsibility for ourselves. The grievance culture makes this harder for us to do and thus threatens one of our most precious capabilities.

Entitlement

'Have you had an accident or been injured in the past three years or assaulted in the last two years? You may be entitled to compensation.' There is nothing particularly unusual in this claim, made by a British firm of personal injury solicitors.[26] Variations of it are made by many such companies. What I find most interesting about it is the use of the language of entitlement. The sense of entitlement encouraged by the grievance culture, with its legalistic discourse, is fundamentally affecting the way we view life's vicissitudes, and much for the worse.

The idea that people's feelings of entitlement are rapidly displacing feelings of gratitude has been articulated by many people for several years now. Mary Warnock, in her book on fertility treatments, lamented the fact that potential parents now see children as a right rather than a blessing.[27] Michael Sandel, arguing about the dangers of genetic enhancement, similarly decried the erosion of the sense of life's giftedness.[28]

It is no coincidence that common to these complaints is a religious form of language that is sounding increasingly alien; 'blessings' are bestowed by the divine, and 'gifts' are from God. No wonder that an increasingly secular society finds it unnatural to think in such terms. But also part of both arguments is the claim that we do not need to subscribe to theological beliefs to have these feelings of thankfulness. All that we need to do is to appreciate the fact that the good things we receive in life are not ours by right but depend on a combination of fortune, circumstance and, sometimes, individual effort.

This is certainly true, but I fear it is nonetheless the case that feelings of gratitude come more naturally to those who hold religious beliefs, while feelings of entitlement are second nature to those who grow up in a secular, consumerist, grievance culture. But while the role of secularism and consumerism in this is widely discussed, the importance of the grievance culture is less widely appreciated.

The decline in religious conviction removed the belief that everything depends on divine grace. This does not logically entail that therefore everything is ours by right, but once you believe that there is no higher authority dishing out life's goods, it is a small psychological step to thinking that you are entitled to anything you want.

This step is harder to take in a society where many people are poor and you see blameless suffering on a daily basis. But as the West got richer, extreme misfortune became the exception rather than the rule. Better diet and medicine increased life-expectancy: an unfortunate phrase, since such figures never indicated that one should really expect to live the average lifespan. But this is what we increasingly do, and to die before the median termination date is seen as an aberration rather than as the natural fate of half the population. And while we still do live, consumerism tells us that we too can have all the material goods and life-enhancing experiences we want.

By themselves, then, secularisation, increased wealth and consumerism diminish the sense in which good fortune is contingent, and make us feel that life's opportunities are there for the taking, and indeed normally should be taken. However, although this takes us close to a feeling of entitlement, arguably it is the rise of the grievance culture which makes entitlement seem like second nature. The progression, crudely, is that the decline of religion makes us believe that we are not dependent on any higher authority for desired goods; consumerism makes us believe that all goods are ours for the taking, should we have the inclination and resources; but it is the grievance culture that makes us feel that we are entitled to have them whatever. This is because in a grievance culture one's own deficiencies are always someone else's fault. If you did badly at school, it is because the system failed to cater for your special educational needs. If you fail in your personal relationships, it is because your parents failed to provide suitable role models for successful loving partnerships. If you fail to become a pop star, it is because friends and family did not believe in you enough. All of this, of course, means that you would have done well at school, had a good relationship or been a pop star if only others had done their part. Hence it is easy to think that you have been robbed of your true entitlement.

However, it is not enough to lament this trend, because much of what lies behind it is highly desirable. It is good that we no longer think of a higher power apportioning fortune according to divine caprice. Indeed, even most intelligent believers in a deity are glad this kind of God is not as worshipped as he once was. It is good that we are wealthier and have more choices. You do hear people claim that we were better-off when we were poor, but most such complainants don't know what it was like back then and wouldn't last one day in a coal-mine or steelworks. It is even good that we have become more aware of the role that education, parents and peers play in our development. Dyslexics, for example, used to be routinely failed by the education system. It is also good that people take parenting more seriously than they used to: the increased role fathers are playing in the upbringing of their children is to me one of the clearest examples of how things have got better, not worse, in recent decades. The problem is that undesirable side-effects seem inexorably to follow from these developments. Raised standards raise expectations.

The grievance culture too has a positive side. To some extent it has been a by-product of the growth of the rights culture. A now standard critique is that rights have been promoted at the expense of responsibility. People see their rights as being unconditional, and this clearly links with a sense of entitlement. While there is something to this criticism, on balance, the promotion of rights following the UN's Universal Declaration has surely been more of a good thing than a bad one. To oppose the entitlement culture does not require hostility to the emphasis on rights in general, merely a recognition that having a right does not absolve you of your duties.

It is also right and proper that people should be held to account for their neglect and wrongdoing. Consider, for example, how children used to suffer beatings and even sexual abuse at the hands of adults in authority over them, in schools and churches. Informal systems failed to safeguard the well-being of these children, and it was therefore right that laws were introduced so that miscreants could be stopped and punished.

Similarly, you would not want to trust to good will alone to make sure landlords keep their gas appliances safe, that concert halls and pubs have sufficient and clear fire exits or that coach operators keep their vehicles safe. Legislation rightly enforces such things, and with this comes the right to sue and seek redress if things go wrong.

The problem, most people say, is that this has simply gone too far. Yes, a pub should have proper fire escapes, but should it be liable for someone slipping on a floor because a punter had spilled her beer? Schools should not beat their pupils, but if routine playground teasing affects a particularly sensitive student badly, is the school guilty of not protecting him against bullying?

If we approach the question from the point of view of responsibility, I think the answers to these questions are not always obvious or clear-cut. And, indeed, this is just how the question is approached in a legalistic culture. But there is another way of looking at social and moral norms, which is to consider the cumulative effect of certain habits or routine practices. This is the approach commended by Aristotle, who argued that human beings are creatures of habit, and that moral development is a matter of inculcating habits conducive to human flourishing.

Foregrounding a sense of entitlement does not help develop such habits. Whereas a sense of gratitude encourages us to locate our own fortune in proper relation to that of others, a sense of entitlement encourages an egocentric view, focused on what is ours by right. Whereas a sense of gratitude makes one more able to deal with life when it doesn't go well, a sense of entitlement leads one to be always dissatisfied at the imperfection of it all. This is fundamental: anyone unable to accept that life isn't perfect is, to my mind, not equipped to be a mature, morally autonomous adult.

An entitlement culture also fosters the view that other people are responsible for meeting your needs, whereas you yourself are usually the person best placed to meet them. Finally, in a world where entitlements compete, as they inevitably will, we will tend to take a defensive attitude to taking on responsibility, because we will fear what people will demand of us if we do.

All these are reasons for wanting to organise society in such a way that entitlement does not become the habitual concept we reach for when understanding our relationship to the world. However, there are signs that this is exactly what too many do already. Young people increasingly expect to have designer clothes, the latest gadgets and, when they are older, a car. Women's magazines sell the idea that a woman is entitled to great sex, regular orgasms, love and respect. Men's magazines also present great sex, great bodies (their own and women's) and great gadgets as the birthright of any fertile young male.

If this is indeed a pernicious trend, how can we curb it? Not, I think, by denying the internal logic of legal responsibility, but by rejecting the whole framework as an inappropriate basis for social interaction. We should not throw out all legislation that holds people to account, but when it comes to difficult grey areas, we should err on the side of risk. Life is inherently perilous, and if we create a society in which we attempt to legislate danger out of existence, we create a false sense, not of security, but of entitlement to good fortune.

The return to ethics

The overall thrust of my argument about the grievance culture is that it places law above ethics, and this leads to three bad consequences: responsibility being denied in some places and inappropriately ascribed in others; a self-imposed curtailment of freedom through fear of litigation and intolerance of risk; and an impoverished culture of entitlement. The obvious conclusion would therefore be to advocate a rejection of legalistic thinking about social norms and to encourage a return to ethics instead. I think this is right, but it is far from clear how it could be achieved.

What we cannot and should not have is a return to authority-based morality. Politically and socially this will not work, since the world has become far too pluralistic for any authority to hold sway in a sustainable way. In the West this is obvious: even the USA, the most religious of all developed countries, has a tremendous diversity of religious denominations, none of which acknowledges the authority of the others. But even in the 'Islamic world', as it is sweepingly called, it is not clear that strong clerical authority has a future. People are simply exposed to too many foreign influences, and when people see choices, they start to choose for themselves.

Iran is a fascinating case in point. I have never been to the country, but you only have to see the films that have come out of it and read stories from people who live there to see that this theocratic country also has a strong secular current in its culture. A small but revealing example is Jafar Panahi's film

Offside, which showed the attempts of some girls to get into an all-male stadium to watch the national football team. It sounds like a tale of bitter struggle against an authoritarian regime, but what is striking is how few characters show any deep commitment to the theology which justifies the girls' exclusion. It's a feeling you get from many other Iranian films. Whatever the ebbs and flows of theocracy, in the longer run there are reasons to hope that the Middle East too will be unable to base its polity on divine authority.

Setting the Middle East aside, in the West this is already an incontrovertible fact. There is no chance of a reversal because the major religions are and will remain Christian, and the authority of organised Christianity is spent. The worldwide Anglican Communion has revealed itself to be the most thoroughgoing relativist religion of all. It embraces African bishops who think homosexuality is an abomination and south London clerics who openly live with their boyfriends. When it rejected its centuries-long ban on women clergy, it tacitly acknowledged that it was now following a moral agenda set by others (thankfully) and no longer leading it.

The Roman Catholic Church likes to present itself as a rock, compared to this wishy-washy Protestant malleability, but the history of that Church also leaves any claims it has to moral authority in tatters. It may move more slowly, but its views have also varied according to history and fashion, with the liberalising agenda of the Second Vatican Council of 1962–65 being largely reversed during the papacy of John Paul II. Its history is full of ignominy, including the Borgias, paedophile priests (and a reluctance to deal with them) and the virtual imprisonment and abuse of girls deemed immoral on spurious grounds in Ireland. Whatever good the Church may have done, it has simply done too much that is bad for it to command any moral authority with any but the most devout of its members.

Evangelical Christianity is even more bankrupt because it claims to take its authority from the Bible. But anyone with even a cursory knowledge of Bible history will realise that this is not a document effectively dictated by God but a very human book, written by various people with different agendas, several decades (and sometimes centuries), after the events they profess to describe. For hundreds of years the books of the New Testament co-existed with many others now deemed heretical, and nothing in the manner of their canonisation suggests that God was in charge of the process. It is a mystery why any intelligent person would think that 'the Bible says' is a moral argument for anything. Yet this is what Evangelical Christians standardly do think. The idea that the majority of the population will ever buy this is frankly absurd.

The obvious alternative is that the return to ethics should be secular in nature. The problem is that secular ethics has so far utterly failed to win the hearts and minds of the masses. At best, it leaves people with a set of limpid platitudes such as 'you should treat people decently'; at worst, it has led to a widespread acceptance of the most vapid and pernicious form of relativism, in which 'there's no right or wrong, it's just whatever you think'.

Moral philosophy has the potential to be a help or a hindrance in this regard, and the way the subject is usually taught, it looks more like a hindrance. Most people who study it are presented with a standard trio of moral frameworks: consequentialism, deontology and virtue ethics. On this view, consequentialists believe that actions are right or wrong solely in terms of whether they produce good or bad outcomes; deontologists believe that some acts are right or wrong in themselves, regardless of their consequences; and virtue theorists say that being good is not about following strict rules but about developing the moral character to make ethical choices. To give these caricatures a concrete example, consequentialists would say that whether torture is wrong depends on whether, on balance, it leads to more goods than harms; a deontologist would say that torture is wrong in itself; and a virtue theorist would say that torture is not something one can imagine a virtuous person doing, but who knows, there may be exceptions.

Of course, these are very crude summaries, but someone studying moral philosophy probably ends their course with the take-home message that moral theory is pretty much like this. The question then becomes, which view is right? There is absolutely no consensus on this, and I think it would take a brave philosopher to say there ever will be. So just as the plurality of moral authorities leaves all of them emaciated, so the plurality of secular moral frameworks leaves no one of them able to command widespread assent. Hence there is nothing to facilitate the kind of return to ethics that can fill the vacuum left by the decline of traditional morality more convincingly than legalism.

However, there is another way of looking at moral philosophy which has more potential. Although there is no consensus as to which moral theory is the right one, there is a tacit acceptance of a common procedure for thinking through moral theories. This can be summed up as the view that moral discourse is a democratic, rational activity. It works by assessing the different reasons given for or against a particular course of action in a way that defers to no authority. This is the way in which ethics committees work: they do not require everyone involved to subscribe to the same fundamental theory of ethics. Rather, they demand that people effectively set these aside and offer only such reasons as can be assessed and judged by the common standards of rationality. It is democratic, not in the sense that it necessarily follows majority opinion, but in the sense that contributions to the debate are assessed on the merits of the arguments, not on the status of the person offering them.

Where univocality is required, a consensus has to be reached which leaves many parties unsatisfied. For example, society has to decide on the legal status of abortion. People's fundamental commitments on this are just incompatible: Catholics regard it as murder, whereas many others defend a mother's right to choose. However, a nation has either to ban or to allow it: there has to be one law which applies to everyone. A Catholic on an ethics committee or commission will therefore probably find themselves on the losing side of the debate. Nevertheless, just as long as everyone can see the general value of democratic, rational debate for resolving such matters in a pluralistic society, this has to be swallowed.

The fact of pluralism means that, whenever univocality is not essential, plurality should be allowed as much as possible. Shops can open on Sundays if they wish, and those who think it impious to go to them can stay at home. Your religion can ban blasphemy, but civil society will not. You may think living together outside marriage is wrong, but the law will not condemn those who choose to do so. This is not the kind of lazy relativism that says morality is just whatever you think it is; it is simply a recognition of two facts about morality. The first is a contingent one: as a matter of fact, reasonable people do not agree on fundamental moral values. In the absence of consensus it is more reasonable to allow as much diversity of opinion as is compatible with a cohesive, workable polis. The second is a more fundamental one: moral values are plural, and there is more than one way of living a good life. This is more contentious, but I think it is reasonable to hypothesise that we will never find one way of living, one way of ordering society, which is best for everyone. Some genuine goods push out other equally legitimate ones. A more mobile society is also a less cohesive one, but can we ever say, once and for all, that mobility trumps cohesion or vice versa? The alternative is to allow different societies, or parts of them, to embody these different goods. For instance, cities celebrate the value of diversity and mobility, while smaller towns may embody the values of stability and cohesion.

Such a pluralist society can nevertheless have a strong ethical culture, just as long as it is widely recognised that decisions about what is right and wrong, whether collective or individual, are based on the rational giving and assessing of reasons. It does not matter that we disagree over what the most fundamental moral values are, as long as we agree that there is a meaningful procedure for talking about and resolving questions of ethics.

How might such an ethical society be nurtured? Education plays a role. There has been enthusiastic talk of 'philosophy for children' programmes in recent years, much of it confused because it misunderstands what this usually involves. I think the description is misleading: children are not being taught philosophy but are being taught how to talk about issues and values together, respecting different opinions and coming to collective decisions. In contrast, philosophy is, more often than not, a gladiatorial contest in which the aim is to emerge as the last one standing in a vicious war of words and logic.

Even if 'philosophy for children' is a misnomer, it does have a part to play in facilitating the return to ethics I favour.

It should be tried, because the alternative is too grim. What are the lessons about ethics that most of us left school having learned? First, that rules are set by grown-ups and you follow them because you have to – but without teachers anything is permitted. Second, that different religions have different moral outlooks and (if you're lucky) so do different philosophers – so you just choose the one you fancy, or choose none, since clearly none is right. Third, there's no real truth about ethics because you've learned that everyone has different views, but you're also told to respect them all – young people thus enter adult life with no sense that ethics is meaningful or rigorous. Fourth, there is no sense of any connection between 'morality' and what it means for one's own life to go well – morality is too often seen as a set of checks on individual behaviour, all about what thou shalt not do. As such, it is seen as a constraint, something perhaps to get around and not something that is needed to help us make decisions to make our own lives flourish.

Compare what might happen if rational discourse about ethics were not just taught but embodied in the ways school work. Children who leave school having had this kind of education will have learned that moral claims require the giving of reasons, and that even though consensus is not always possible, agreement sometimes has to be reached for practical purposes. On other occasions each can freely pursue his or her own conception of the good life. More importantly, ethics would seem relevant. The reason-giving nature of ethical discourse constantly forces us to say why it is good for us and for others that we do certain actions rather than others. Morality ceases to be primarily about holding us back and instead becomes a precondition of going forward in positive ways.

A generation of citizens who have had this educational

experience might just be equipped to reject the current legalism which is keeping warm the seat of ethics vacated by the old moral authorities. I can't pretend that I'm completely confident that this will work. We often expect too much of education, when it is the wider culture that really has to change. But at the same time, in practice, much of the culture of ethics I advocate is already in place. Not just in ethics committees but also in public forums such as debates and the serious media we expect people to give reasons for the values they profess and to have these interrogated. What is needed is not therefore a radical change but a shift of power, so that this, rather than legalism, becomes the dominant paradigm within which people think about their responsibilities and the morality of their actions.

The grievance culture is a weed which has driven out its fairer relative, moral complaint. There are other ways of trying to prune it, but if we want to attack it at its roots, we need the soil of ethics, not law.

CONCLUSION

I said at the beginning of this book that my aim was to counter the perception we have of complaint as negative, trivial and largely pointless with the idea that it can be a positive, constructive force, springing from the very essence of what makes us human. At its noblest, complaint – as a directed expression of a refusal or inability to accept that things are not as they ought to be – lies at the very heart of all campaigns to create a better, more just world. At its worst, wrong complaint is manifest in a grievance culture which undermines ethics and replaces it with a legalistic set of attitudes which undermines responsibility, freedom and a proper sense of life's contingencies.

But even at a less grand level, being more sensitive to the difference between right and wrong complaint can make numerous small differences to our lives. It can be a terrible waste of energy to complain about those things which either cannot or should not be changed. Inevitably, many if not most of our complaints are of this kind, but as long as we accept that venting our spleens in such cases is no more than a cathartic release, or even a leisure activity we enjoy, this is not a problem. Troubles arise when such complaints lead to frustration and stress as we fail to realise the functional pointlessness of our protests.

It is also helpful to be more conscious of the manner, as well as of the matter, of our complaining. There is no requirement for complaints to be born of anger, or for them to be made rudely. The art of constructive complaint requires knowing when a calm approach is more likely to restore things to how they ought to be, and when a flying rage is the only thing likely to force the issue. It also requires being specific and proportionate in what we complain about.

There is also some value in reflecting on what our complaints say about ourselves, as individuals as well as generations, nations and perhaps sexes: you shall know us by our complaints. Complaint is not unique in this respect: to a certain degree, almost anything we say or do in particular reflects something more general. But complaint seems to me to be particularly revealing and interesting, partly because it is not usually considered worthy of serious examination and partly because complaining is one of the most human things we do.

It is this which, I think, makes complaint so important. So much of life is about dealing with the gap between how things are and how we think they ought to be. How much imperfection must we accept, and how much should we strive to change? It's a question we face every day, with jobs, friends, partners, our bodies and minds, and in politics and social justice. It is hardly a distortion to say that such questions are effectively about whether we should complain or persevere, about whether we direct our dissatisfaction at others or whether we need to take responsibility ourselves, and how we put these decisions into practice.

General policies are no substitute here for wise judgement. People who habitually keep their complaints to themselves can be even harder to deal with than those who complain too much: at least with the latter you know what they think. However, having thought about the nature of right and wrong complaint at least gives us the background to make more reflective judgements.

Do not, then, believe those who say we would do better to

complain less, not only because these are often the very people who have most to gain by the status quo being unchallenged but also because it is the quality rather than the quantity of our complaining which counts. To echo Martin Luther King, I do not therefore say 'Get rid of your discontent'. Rather, I have tried to say that this normal and healthy discontent can be channelled into the creative outlet of constructive, positive complaint and action to bring the world closer to how it ought to be.

APPENDIX

THE COMPLAINT SURVEY

The survey I discuss in Chapter 4 was conducted at this book's web site, www.thecomplaintbook.com. Of the many people who took the survey, only the results of the 920 who completed all of it have been used in the analysis. This appendix includes a partial summary of the main results.

This is what is known as a self-selecting survey, which means that people were not selected to reflect a representative spread of the population but volunteered themselves to answer questions. As such, they are highly unreliable in many respects. Most importantly, the brute totals recorded by the survey should not be taken as an accurate reflection of the population as a whole.

Nevertheless, such surveys can be more indicative of general trends when you look at *relative* answers. For example, it would be unlikely (but not impossible) if the variations in responses which emerge only when you factor in age were artefacts of anything other than age. Whatever the social mix of people who took the survey, if older participants responded systematically differently from younger ones, then that difference is probably a product of either age per se or of shifts in values and beliefs that have occurred between generations. Hence in presenting these results I have in general given relative, not absolute, data.

One final caveat: it is not my belief that any claim made in this book is proven or even made likely by this survey. At most it suggests things which may be true, but whether those things are right is something we must either judge for ourselves or find the harder evidence to back it up.

Table 1: What do people complain about most?

Participants were asked to say whether they 'complain very regularly', 'complain quite often', 'complain from time to time' or 'rarely complain' about thirteen common subjects for complaint. The resulting 'complaint factor' is represented as a percentage, where 100 would represent all participants saying they complained very regularly and 0 saying they rarely complained. The number in brackets represents the difference in the complaint factor compared with results when people were asked what they thought *other people* in their country complained about. In every case but one, people judged their own level of complaint to be higher than that of others. The only thing people thought others complained about more than they did themselves was 'religious leaders'.

1	Bad luck or fate	85	(+14)
2	Personal ill health	80	(+22)
3	How things have generally got worse	73	(+31)
4=	Spouses/partners/friends	73	(+18)
	The weather	68	(+33)
6	Religious leaders	63	(-8)
7=	The cost of living	60	(+28)
	Public transport	60	(+21)
9=	Corrupt politicians	59	(+16)
	Television	59	(+9)
	Poor-quality goods	59	(+5)
12	Poor service	51	(+6)
13	Ineffective politicians	48	(+18)
	Average	64	(+16)

Table 2: What do people complain about in the UK and USA?

Figures here represent the difference in 'complaint factor' scores (calculated as for Table 1) between the USA and the UK, where a plus score indicates a higher UK level of complaint and a minus score a higher level of US complaint. Note that although there are wide variations on specific complaints, the average is remarkably similar.

Corrupt politicians	+21	UK
Religious leaders	+12	
Ineffective politicians	+8	
How things have generally got worse	+7	
Television	+5	
Bad luck or fate	+2	
Personal ill health	-2	
Spouses/partners/friends	-4	
Poor-quality goods	-5	
The cost of living	-7	
Poor service	-13	
The weather	-13	
Public transport	-29	USA
Average	-2	

Table 3: How do people complain in the UK and USA?

Figures here represent the percentage of respondents who chose the statement as being more true of their country than the alternative in the pair.

	UK	USA
People tend to complain to others if they are not happy	71	90
People tend to keep their complaints to themselves	29	10
People believe the point of complaint is to change things	12	24
People don't believe complaining often changes anything	88	76
When people complain, they try to be very polite	50	15
When people complain, they tend to show their anger or irritation	50	85
People who complain are admired for their openness or courage	16	17
People who complain are looked down on as negative and miserable	84	83
People tend to complain to the people responsible for their grievance	12	25
People tend to complain among their friends, but not to the people with power to change things	88	75

Table 4: What do men and women complain about?

Figures here represent the difference in scores (calculated as for Table 1) between men and women, where a plus score indicates a higher female level of complaint and a minus score a higher level of male complaint. Note that there is less variation here than there is in Table 2, which compared national differences. Note also how the average level of complaint is again very similar.

Religious leaders	+13	Female
Television	+10	
Ineffective politicians	+8	
Corrupt politicians	+4	
Poor-quality goods	−2	
How things have generally got worse	−3	
Bad luck or fate	−5	
Poor service	−5	
Public transport	−6	
Personal ill health	−8	
The weather	−11	
Spouses/partners/friends	−12	
The cost of living	−13	Male
Average	−2	

Table 5: What difference does age make?

This graph shows how levels of self-reported complaint varied with age for those subjects where clear trends were evident. The two types of complaint about politicians have been combined into one for this graph. The thick grey line running through the middle is the average complaint factor.

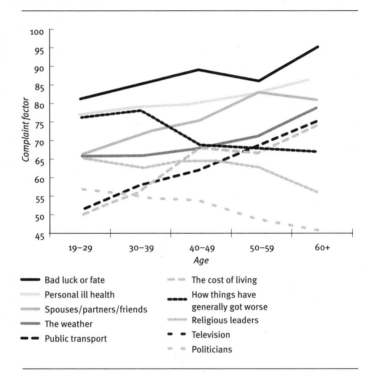

FURTHER READING

Epicurus, *The Epicurus Reader: Selected Writings and Testimonia* (Hackett, 1994)

Desiderius Erasmus, *The Complaint of Peace* (1517)

David Walter Hall, *The Last Priest* (Lulu.com, 2007)

Charles F. Hanna, 'Complaint as a Form of Association', *Qualitative Sociology*, vol. 4, no. 4 (December 1981)

Robert Hughes, *Culture of Complaint: The Fraying of America* (Oxford University Press, 1993)

Martin Luther King, *A Call to Conscience: The Landmark Speeches of Dr. Martin Luther King, Jr.*, ed. Clayborne Carson and Kris Shepard (Warner Books, 2002)

Jack Kornfield (ed.), *Teachings of the Buddha* (Shambhala Publications, 1996)

Robin M. Kowalski, 'Complaints, and Complaining: Functions, Antecedents and Consequences', *Psychological Bulletin*, vol. 119, no. 2 (1996)

Robin M. Kowalski, *Complaining, Teasing, and Other Annoying Behaviors* (Yale University Press, 2003)

Michael J. Sandel, *The Case against Perfection: Ethics in the Age of Genetic Engineering* (Harvard University Press, 2007)

Henry David Thoreau, *Civil Disobedience* (1849)

Mary Woollstonecraft, *A Vindication of the Rights of Woman* (1792)

ACKNOWLEDGEMENTS

Thanks to: series editor Lisa Appignanesi, Daniel Crewe and Andrew Franklin at Profile for helping to develop the idea for the book, commissioning it and offering numerous excellent suggestions; Lizzy Kremer for continuing advice and encouragement; Robin M. Kowalski and Charles F. Hanna for sharing their knowledge of work on complaint in psychology and sociology respectively; Gavin McLaughlin at Netspace and Mike Baker at Aileach Design for the book's web site and survey; everyone who took part in the survey; Dorset Humanists and Burnham Philosophical Society for comments on work in progress; David Walter Hall for information about Jean Meslier; Matt Seaton at *Comment is Free*; Maureen Rice at *Psychologies*; and above all to Antonia Macaro for reading and commenting on the draft, and not complaining about how much time I spent working on it.

NOTES

1. Academic research in the area of complaint is scarce, except in the case of consumer complaint. Exceptions to this rule are the excellent popular book *Complaining, Teasing, and Other Annoying Behaviors* (Yale University Press, 2003) and the academic paper 'Complaints, and Complaining: Functions, Antecedents and Consequences' (*Psychological Bulletin*, vol. 119, no. 2, 1996), by the psychologist Robin M. Kowalski, and the paper 'Complaint as a Form of Association' (*Qualitative Sociology*, vol. 4, no. 4, December 1981) by the sociologist Charles F. Hanna.

2. David Walter Hall, *The Last Priest*. Hall also includes an actual passage from Meslier's Testament (Gourmelon translation): 'This is what gives all these gentlemen the means to entertain themselves and have all kinds of amusement, while you the poor, abused by the faults and superstitions of religion, groan sadly, poorly and without protest under the yoke of the oppression of the great.'

3. See Michael Onfray, *In Defence of Atheism: The Case against Christianity, Judaism and Islam* (Serpent's Tail, 2007), esp. p.195.

4. *Dhammapada* (124), trans. Juan Mascaró (Penguin, 1973).

5. From *Majjihma Nikaya*, in *Teachings of the Buddha*, ed. Jack Kornfield (Shambhala Publications, 1996), p.74.

6. From *Vissuddhimagga*, in Kornfield (ed.), op. cit., p.18.

7. From *Dhammapada*, in Kornfield (ed.), op. cit., p.15.

8. All passages from *The Koran*, trans. N.J. Dawood (Penguin, 1974).

9. 'Noble or Savage?', *Economist* (19 December 2007).
10. Frans de Waal, *Our Inner Ape* (Granta, 2005).
11. Summary of LAAG response to airport planning application, 26 April 2007, posted at www.kentnet.org.uk/laag/Planning%20Application-LAAG%20Response-summary.pdf
12. *Environmental News Daily*, issue 690 (31 January 2000).
13. George Orwell, *The Road to Wigan Pier* (Penguin, 2001), pp.88–9.
14. National Statistics Online, www.statistics.gov.uk/cci/nugget.asp?id=934
15. Presentation given 30 March 2004, www.cabinetoffice.gov.uk/strategy/downloads/files/lifechances_socialmobility.pdf
16. BBC News Online (3 September 2007), http://news.bbc.co.uk/2/hi/uk_news/education/6972699.stm
17. The text of this interview is widely available online, for example at http://news.bbc.co.uk/1/hi/uk_politics/2726831.stm
18. 'Morality? Don't Make Me Laugh', *The Guardian* (20 April 1999). See www.johnpilger.com/page.asp?partid=203
19. Slavoj Žižek, interviewed in *What More Philosophers Think*, ed. J. Baggini and J. Stangroom (Continuum, 2007).
20. George W. Bush's speech to the American Enterprise Institute, 23 February 2003, www.pbs.org/newshour/bb/middle_east/iraq/bush_2-26.html
21. Prime Minister's statement on Iraq, 25 February 2003, www.pm.gov.uk/output/Page3088.asp
22. See 'Blair: Saddam Most Dangerous Leader', CNN.com (20 February 2001), http://edition.cnn.com/2001/WORLD/europe/UK/02/20/bush.blair/

23. See Robin M. Kowalski, *Complaining, Teasing, and Other Annoying Behaviors* (Yale University Press, 2003).

24. Robert Hughes, *Culture of Complaint: The Fraying of America*, (Oxford University Press, 1993).

25. Michael Power, *The Risk Management of Everything: Rethinking the Politics of Uncertainty* (Demos, 2004).

26. www.accidentclaimscountrywide.co.uk/services.html, accessed 12/11/07.

27. Mary Warnock, *Making Babies: Is There a Right to Have Children?* (Oxford University Press, 2002).

28. Michael J Sandel, *The Case against Perfection: Ethics in the Age of Genetic Engineering* (Harvard University Press, 2007).

INDEX